Town and City Histories

Blackburn

TOWN AND CITY HISTORIES
HISTORICAL EDITOR: STEPHEN CONSTANTINE

BLACKBURN

The Development of a Lancashire Cotton Town

Derek Beattie

*Illustrated from the archives
and with contemporary photographs by*
IAN BEESLEY

Ryburn Publishing

First Published in 1992
Ryburn Publishing Limited
Krumlin, Halifax

Composed by Ryburn Publishing Services
Origination by Ryburn Reprographics
Bound in Bodmin, Cornwall, by Hartnolls
Printed by Ryburn Book Production,
Halifax, England

Town and City Histories
ISSN 0952-6153

Blackburn
ISBN 1-85331-021-2

Contents

Historical Editor's Foreword

The books in this series are designed and written with a broad readership in mind: local people interested to know how the character of their town has been shaped by major historical forces and the energies of their predecessors; newcomers and visitors curious to acquire a historical introduction to their new surroundings; general readers wishing to see how the sweeps of national and international history have manifested themselves in particular urban communities; and the scholar seeking to understand urbanisation by comparing and contrasting local experiences.

We live, most of us, in intensely urban environments. These are the products largely of the last two centuries of historical development, although the roots of many towns, of course, go back deep into the past. In recent years there has been considerable historical research of a high standard into this urban history. Narrative and descriptive accounts of the history of towns and cities can now be replaced by studies such as the TOWN AND CITY HISTORIES which investigate, analyse and, above all, explain the economic, political, social and cultural processes and consequences of urbanisation.

Writers for this series consider the changing economic foundations of their town or city and the way change has affected its physical shape, built environment, employment opportunities and urban character. The nature and interests of those who wielded power locally and the structure and functions of local government in different periods are also examined, since locally exercised authority could determine much about the fortunes and quality of urban life. Particular emphasis is placed on the changing life experiences of ordinary men, women and children – their homes, education, occupations, social relations, living standards and leisure activities. Towns and cities control and respond to the values, aspirations and actions of their residents. The books in this series therefore explore social behaviour as well as the economic and political history of those who lived in and helped make the towns and cities of today.

Stephen Constantine
University of Lancaster

Dedication

To my wife Judith and my daughters
Emma, Cordelia and Naomi

Acknowledgements

My thanks to the staff of Blackburn Museum, Blackburn Library, Blackburn College Library and Lancaster University Library. My greatest debt, however, is to Dr. Stephen Constantine who not only invited me to write this book but, as both editor of this series and my former doctoral supervisor, has taught me most of what little I know of writing History. His constant attention to detail never ceases to amaze me, whilst his patience appears unlimited and his encouragement unceasing.

I also owe thanks to my wife, daughters and friends whose persistent question 'Have you finished your book yet?' has kept me working.

This book could not have been written without the efforts of all those former students whose research I have called upon so widely. They also I thank. Since not all who read this book will necessarily agree with my views I must stress that they are entirely mine.

Derek Beattie
Blackburn, August 1992

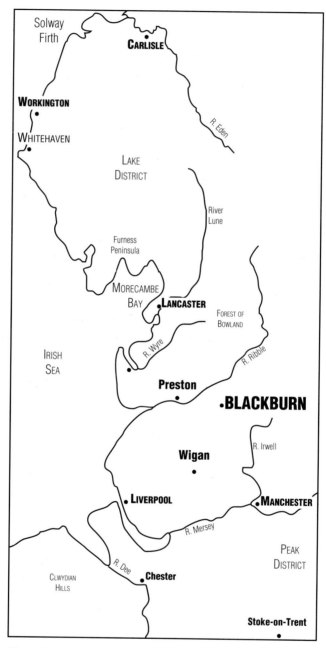

Map of north-west England

1

Blackburn to 1750:
the town that History passed by

In 1880 Blackburn had a population of over 100,000. Just over one hundred years before it had an estimated population of only 5,000. Blackburn's importance as a town, therefore, is relatively recent. Cotton brought about the change. The growth of the cotton industry was the reason for Blackburn's rise from obscurity. Without cotton the town's growth would not have been so rapid or so great. It is important to realise this fact, because when the reason for a town's growth is based on one industry, once that industry declines so may the town.

Blackburn sits in the valley of the river Blakewater which drains from the Rossendale uplands, a western spur of the Pennine hills that lie to the east of the town. The river joins the Darwen which runs from the south east to the north west along the south-western outskirts of the town. With an average rainfall of 45 inches there are ample supplies of soft water draining from the local gritstone. In the surrounding area there were also plentiful supplies of local coal.[1]

Blackburn's earliest beginnings are shrouded. It is known that Blackburn stands where the Roman military road from Mamucium (Manchester) crossed the river Blakewater on its way to nearby Bremetennacum (Ribchester), but whether settlement or road came first is unclear. What is also known is that the Romans did not feel it important enough to build a base here, preferring to construct a fort further north on the banks of the river Ribble.

Why Blackburn is even called Blackburn is a mystery. In the small paragraph that the Domesday Book deigned to devote to the entire Blackburn Hundred it is spelt Blacheborne. Is its root an old English word meaning 'to bleach'? The original bleaching process needed plentiful water so perhaps Blackburn's site was decided by the textile industry from the very beginning. Or is the name simply derived from Black burn or stream?

It has already been noted that the Romans came, looked and chose Ribchester: a case of *veni, vidi, ivi*. The Saxons did at least stay, which is more than the Normans did, Roger de Poitou choosing to build his castle at

Clitheroe, a dozen miles to the north east in the Ribble valley. To the Saxons Blackburn owes the original parish church of St. Mary's, suggesting the existence of at least a small nuclear township. But even then future servants of God chose to pass by on the other side of the road. The Cistercian monks picked nearby Whalley for the site of their abbey in 1178. Even the supposed followers of Satan seemed to shun the town. In 1612, of the nineteen witches sent for trial at Lancaster castle from this area none were from Blackburn.

The Wars of the Roses came and went. It may have been the House of Lancaster fighting against the House of York but apparently no-one told the inhabitants of Blackburn to become involved. The only nearby excitement occurred in 1464 when Henry VI was caught whilst trying to escape from Waddington Hall in the adjacent Ribble valley.

Blackburn failed to sleep through the English Civil War, though not for the want of trying. Of the six 'Hundreds' that comprised Lancashire four elected to support the cause of King Charles whilst one sided with Parliament. Blackburn was the exception; it was unsure and uncommitted. Outsiders, however, ensured that Blackburn did become involved. The first action occurred in October 1642 when the royalist Sir Gilbert Hoghton of Hoghton Tower, lying to the west of the town, successfully seized a weapon store held at Whalley Abbey and then prepared to settle down for the night in Blackburn whilst on his way home. His forces were surprised by 200 parliamentarian soldiers led by Colonel Shuttleworth of Gawthorpe Hall near Burnley, and the evening of 27th October saw fighting along Darwen Street and Church Street and Hoghton force's fleeing.

The second action occurred on Christmas eve of the same year. Hoghton returned, set up a small cannon near Bank House at the top of Dukes Brow and opened fire. The only casualty was a frying pan. Not wishing to miss their Christmas festivities the besiegers then left to return to Hoghton Tower. Other than that eminently forgettable skirmish the remainder of the civil war passed Blackburn by except that Prince Rupert rode through on his way to the battle of Marston Moor. He lost. The only lasting result of these years was the destruction of the market cross by rowdy parliamentarian soldiers. It was never repaired and for years to come the 'Blackburn Stump' sat next to the stocks and well where Church Street, Darwen Street, King Street and Northgate met.

Blackburn's strategic isolation was seen again in the Jacobite Rebellions of 1715 and 1745. Though Preston was occupied for the Stuarts in 1715 no march on Blackburn was made. The nearest anyone came was when a forage party penetrated as far as Darwen via Tockholes. A Captain Aynesworth of Pleasington had organised barricades across Blackburn's streets but they were not needed.

In 1745 Preston was again occupied for the Stuart cause as Bonnie Prince Charlie marched his highlander followers south. Sir Henry Hoghton now left his tower and visited Blackburn to organise the local levies in defence of the Hanoverian succession. On hearing that the rebels might be advancing on Blackburn he sensibly decided to march in the opposite direction. He need not have bothered. The Jacobites carried on southwards. They even failed to visit Blackburn on their eventual retreat.

It was no accident that Blackburn was an historical backwater throughout these centuries. Since it was not on any major north–south route, nor was it on a main east–west route, Blackburn was never of strategic importance to anyone. It was merely a relatively isolated market town that had quietly risen to be the main market town for north-east Lancashire. It served its hinterland and asked for no more or less.

As farming land, the surrounding area was never rich, and local farmers, certainly as far back as the thirteenth century, had always weaved as a second income. The cloth they produced was sold to clothiers or chapmen who took it to surrounding markets. It was through these men, many of yeoman stock, that towns such as Blackburn, Burnley, Accrington, Nelson and Colne began to specialise more and more in textiles. In these free or non-corporate towns, not controlled by the guilds, anyone could set up in trade and they did.

Blackburn by Elizabethan times was noted for its woollen cloth, though by the time of the Stuarts it had shifted to linen. During Cromwell's Protectorate, Blackburn Checks came to the fore. This cloth had a linen warp and a cotton weft and one or both were dyed to give it its distinctive check appearance. Blue and white became the pattern most associated with Blackburn: colours still sported by the town's soccer club, Blackburn Rovers. Alongside this cloth was produced Blackburn Greys, a plain unfinished cloth. Blackburn's resultant reliance on the textile industry can be seen by a study of the parish registry of 1723. Of the 149 baptism entries, 68 were children of weavers. Of the 60 burial entries, 34 heads of families were weavers.[2] Textiles were already the major industry. The scene was set for Blackburn to arise from obscurity as the industrial revolution, led by cotton, got under way. How Blackburn and its people adapted to the sudden onrush of rapid urbanisation is the subject of the following chapters.

REFERENCES

1. My thanks to Dave Pack of the Geography department at Blackburn College for the geographical details.
2. W. A. Abram, *A History of the Blackburn Parish*, J. G. & J. Toulmin, Blackburn, 1877.

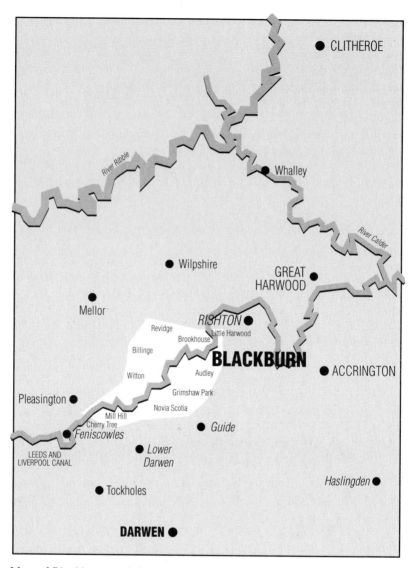

Map of Blackburn and district

2

The economy
1750–1914

As we have seen, Blackburn was already noted for textiles by 1750. Textile manufacture in the form of cotton cloth thereafter expanded rapidly and Blackburn expanded with it. The cotton industry was at first dominated by cotton merchants supplying the domestic system of manufacture. These merchants purchased the raw cotton and took it to cottagers who spun it first into thread and then wove it into cloth. They were paid by the piece. The merchants then had the cloth bleached and dyed in buildings that spread along the River Blakewater. Calico printing using wooden blocks was initially used in the town then cylinder printing began to replace this from 1775. Then came the spinning mills followed by those housing the power looms. The age of the domestic system of manufacture was replaced by the factory.

> For years cotton merchants flourished so exceedingly in Blackburn, and such fabulous fortunes were amassed in a short time, there was a general rush to get into it .... The trade in a very short time not only absorbed the whole town but spread out into the country districts around, and the banks of the Blakewater are covered with great mills right up the valley to Accrington.[1]

By the end of the nineteenth century Blackburn had become the cotton weaving capital of the world. By 1914 the town was at its peak both in terms of population and industrial output (see Table 1 overleaf).

The first mills in Blackburn were spinning mills and were converted warehouses. The first purpose built spinning mill was constructed at Wensley Fold in 1797. By 1816 there were nine mills in the parish but still only one in the town itself. Delayed by earlier machine breaking rampages by domestic spinners, the opening of spinning mills using the latest machines only accelerated at the end of the Napoleonic wars. There were 24 by 1824 employing 10,460 hands. By 1831, 15,000 spinners looked after 170,000 spindles. 1849 saw the town boast 1.1 million spindles.[2] Spinning's zenith in Blackburn was reached in 1870. Prior to that 24 new spinning

Table 1   Population Statistics

Year	Population
1780	5,000 est.
1801	11,980
1811	15,083
1821	21,940
1831	27,091
1841	36,000
1851	46,538
1861	63,126
1871	76,339
1881	104,012
1891	120,064
1901	129,216
1911	133,052
1921	129,400
1931	122,971

mills had been built in the previous twenty years. Decline then set in. From 2.5 million spindles the industry returned to 1.1 million by 1900. During that thirty-year period sixteen spinning mills either closed down or converted to weaving. Only four new ones replaced them, and even joint spinning and weaving mills fell from 45 to 29 over that same period.[3] The spinning industry moved to South Lancashire especially Bolton and Oldham. In its place came the rise to dominance of the power loom and the weaving mill.

The first mill to introduce power looms was Bannister Eccles Dandy Mill at Grimshaw Park. Originally built in 1820 for spinning, it installed power looms in 1825. Though Richard Cartwright had invented the power loom back in 1785, it is estimated that by 1820 there were only 14,500 in the whole of Britain. Technical difficulties inhibited its sales. The first commercially and technically successful power loom was that of Roberts and Sharp which was marketed in 1822. The use of this type of loom now mushroomed though not initially in North Lancashire and not in Blackburn. In the first official census of power looms, made in 1835 by the newly appointed factory inspectors, out of 61,176 looms in Lancashire only 12,000 were in North Lancashire and just 3,200 in Blackburn.[4] Other than the technical problems that beset Cartwright's loom, memories of early machine-breaking riots in Blackburn, coupled with a still plentiful and cheap supply of handloom weavers, meant that the main expansion of power looms in this town was delayed until after the mid 1840s.

The two decades between 1850–1870 saw the acceleration of weaving in Blackburn with 68 new weaving-only mills built in the town and four combined mills. This followed the invention of the Kenworthy power loom by a group of weaver engineers at the local Brookhouse mill. The cloth that could be produced by this loom was of a far higher quality than had been possible before on other power looms.

The period 1870–1890 saw nine weaving mills built each decade. Expansion after that, as will be seen, was in the size of the mills rather than in their number. The 48,000 looms in Blackburn in 1870 grew to 88,770 by 1914.[5] The Kenworthy power loom that set this expansion off was one of the last nails in the coffin of the handloom weaver.

Weaving in and around Blackburn in the eighteenth century had been carried out by handloom weavers in their own cottages. Known locally as the 'fested' system, weavers lived in small communities up to six miles from the town in areas such as Little Harwood, Whitebirk, Stanhill and Knuzden. Each weaver worked within the 'putting out' system whereby they signed up with a local cotton merchant such as Robert Hopwood or George Briggs; the latter had up to 800 weavers on his books at one point in time. In 1800 it is estimated that there were more than 20,000 such handloom weavers within a three mile radius of Blackburn. At this time they mainly produced heavy jaconettes, checks and shirting.[6]

Even before the advent of the power loom in Blackburn the handloom weavers were beginning to experience difficulties and a lowering of their standard of living. Overcrowding within their trade, especially after 1815 when men returned from the Napoleonic wars, saw a decline in piece rates from a high point in 1797. There were 170,000 handloom weavers in Lancashire in the 1820s. In the parish of Blackburn alone there were 14,750 in 1821.

As wages declined so, slowly, did the numbers in the domestic side of the industry, especially in and around Blackburn after the belated introduction of the power loom in the town's mills. This economic pincer movement of an overcrowded industry and the advent of new technology not only reduced their number and standard of living but also changed their work. Whilst always involved in the quality end of the market, producing 'fancy' goods and cambrics, this now became the mainstay of their work, retaining that part of the market in which power looms could not yet compete. Even so, by 1838 the number of handloom weavers living in and around Blackburn was estimated at 7,000 and still declining, whilst one source in 1841 claimed that the number had diminished to just over 1,000.[7]

Within the parish of Blackburn this could well be true, but a recent study of the 1851 census returns has shown that in Blackburn's surrounding hamlets handloom weaving still survived.[8] Accurate figures for all parishes are difficult to determine since some census enumerators often failed to differentiate between handloom and powerloom weavers. The figures for Blackburn suggest a minimum of 986 and a maximum of 4,257 handloom weavers, representing anything between 2% and 9% of the working population. The lower of the two figures is probably nearer the true figure since that matches previous estimates. Moving away from the centre of Blackburn, however, the number of handloom weavers remaining slowly increases. In Livesey there were between 180 and 267, representing 7–10% of the working community, whilst at Little Harwood there were 51 representing 16%. A little further out in Ramsgreave the figure was 155 being 35% of the workers, whilst in Wilpshire it was 76 and 32%. Yet further out in the village of Mellor the total was between 371 and 706, representing 22–44%, and in Tockholes it was 219–223 being 24–25%. It appears that in the nearby outlying rural areas around Blackburn handloom weavers not only survived but made up a sizable proportion of the local workforce.

Within Blackburn the handloom weavers tended to congregate in small communities, possibly signed up to the same 'putter out'. In the Mile End area of Blackburn in 1851, out of a total population of 279, of the 162 employed 130 were handloom weavers.[9]

The reason for the survival of such communities is partly that for all the improvements of the power loom it was still more economical for handloom weavers to produce the fine, fancy and mixed cloths. The existence of a cheap and flexible supply of such weavers also gave entrepreneurs the choice of labour intensive or capital intensive production. For men with a modicum of capital 'putting out' was perhaps still a viable alternative to the expense of opening a mill.

Many handloom weavers prolonged their working life by becoming employed in handloom sheds. Most of these were situated in Blackburn itself. They were owned by entrepreneurs, drawn from many walks of life including other handloom weavers, and they represented the halfway stage between the true domestic system and the modern power driven mill, employing weavers working on handlooms but outside their cottages and away from their families. The majority of such sheds employed 10–30 people but with some holding as many as 50–100 weavers. These employees did not own the looms but worked regular hours under supervision.[10] They also tended to be young. Many old handloom weavers saw such work as beneath them while employers found them difficult to train to factory rules. Such sheds were not immediately replaced by the mills and the demise of the handloom weaver was long and drawn out. The last handloom shop stopped production in Blackburn in 1894. The last handloom weaver died in 1921.[11]

Blackburn did have other industries. The main secondary one was engineering though this was geared to the cotton trade, mainly producing textile machinery. It remained, however, quite small when compared to cotton. In 1881 it only employed 6% of the total workforce of the town compared to cotton's 59.7%, a ratio that had hardly altered by 1911.[12] Engineering in many other cotton towns was comparatively far larger. In Bolton and Rochdale the engineering workforce was 50% that of cotton whilst in Oldham it was the same size. The only other industry employing as many people as engineering in Blackburn was building, busily erecting not only the cotton mills but the houses of the ever-growing numbers of cotton workers. Even in a county of cotton towns, Blackburn was singularly a cotton town.

Since it was so dependent on cotton anything that affected that trade affected Blackburn. The result was a series of booms and slumps that continually punctuated the general growth that was seen throughout the

The interior of a shuttle works in Addison street about 1900. Though cotton mills dominated Blackburn, supporting industries grew up to service them and employed many in the town. Their prosperity went hand in hand with the mills. Along with the rest of Blackburn, when cotton prospered they prospered and when cotton suffered they suffered.
Courtesy of Blackburn Library

nineteenth century and up to 1914. The cyclical depressions included 1801, 1809–11, 1826–7, 1835, 1841–43, 1847, 1857, 1878–80, 1882–5, 1892–6, 1903–4 and 1908. All were painful for the employers but even more so for the ordinary working people of Blackburn. The slumps brought with them unemployment, short-time working and fewer looms per worker for those lucky enough still to be employed at all. Even in 1908 those in work found their earnings cut in this way to 10s (50p) per week compared to the normal 24s (£1.20).[13]

Nearly a century earlier in 1826 workers were paying an even harsher price for a fall in the demand for cotton. Blackburn was

> divided into sixteen districts, and Visitors appointed to call at every house, in order to ascertain the wants of the really necessitous poor. The task was a most arduous one to perform, and many were the heartrending scenes of distress which they were compelled to witness. During the last nine weeks about fourteen thousand individuals (more than half the population of the township) have been relieved weekly with food.[14]

In the slump of 1841–43 a soup kitchen had to be set up in the Old Square. 1847 saw the Visitor system set up again and 12,000 people supplied with food to help survive the trade depression.[15] Even in 1908 with 4,000 unemployed in Blackburn, 2,500 had to turn to the Distress Committee for relief.

But the largest, most famous and most distressing depression in Blackburn's history was between 1861–65 during the cotton famine. This was brought about by the American Civil War when the Unionist North blockaded the Confederate South and stopped supplies of raw cotton from reaching Lancashire. But what has to be challenged here is the myth that Blackburn's inhabitants stoically starved in order to help free the southern negro slaves. This is far from the truth. The millowners and seemingly their workers supported the southern Confederate states throughout the American Civil War.[16]

At first Blackburn fully supported military intervention on behalf of the South. 'The sooner we cease to be neutral and become belligerent the better' was the cry.[17] The northern states were blamed for waging an economic war to extend their commercial empire. A Southern Club was founded in the town, and Abraham Lincoln's Emancipation Proclamation was condemned as hypocritical.[18]

Though the call for military intervention on behalf of the Confederacy was relatively shortlived, the continued support for the southern states was not. As late as October 1864 an address was sent in the name of the people of Blackburn to the people of America, through the Governor of New York, asking for an end to the war and the recognition of the South.[19] The rare receipt of southern cotton in the town was always ecstatically welcomed. Richard Hopwood Hopkinson, a local millowner, was said to have made nearly £1,000,000 'by running the (cotton) blockade'.[20]

But the slumps, however distressing they were and for whatever reason they were caused, were but painful hiccups in a general growth to prosperity for the town of Blackburn. That growth brought with it changes in the structure of the town's workforce that were to colour much of its social development.

Child labour had always played a part in textile manufacture. Under the domestic system the family worked as a unit with the children playing the role of assistant to the parents. This pattern was maintained in the early years of the factory system that was dominated by spinning. But with the advent of the power loom the demand for the labour of both women and children grew, especially as weaving slowly came to dominate the economy of Blackburn. Such labour was quite capable of performing many of the tasks required in weaving and had the added attraction of being cheap. As a consequence the practice of child labour was maintained in Blackburn despite the passing of the Factory Acts during the nineteenth century limiting their use. These Acts did bring an end to the employment of the very young and did limit the hours and regulate the working conditions of older children, but as late as 1914 children from the age of twelve were still being employed in the town's mills.

This was due to the half-time system that allowed parents to claim exemption for their children from full-time education after that was made compulsory in Blackburn following the Education Act of 1870. If exemption were granted, then such children could work in the mills the maximum hours allowed by current legislation. Initially children over the age of eight could be freed for mill work. This was raised to ten in the mid 1870s, eleven in 1893 and twelve in 1899. It still remained at twelve in 1914. As will be seen in Chapter 6 the cotton employers, who dominated the committee granting the exemption certificates, encouraged requests and were fully supported by most parents who wanted the extra family income that child labour brought. In 1914 1,600 half-timers still laboured in Blackburn's mills. This resulted in 29.3% of all boys and 29.4% of all girls under 13 in the borough being employed, mostly in cotton.[21] After the age of thirteen was reached full-time working was allowed.

Women were another major source of labour for the town's mills since in terms of wages they too came cheaply. In 1841, when the power looms were being established in Blackburn, there were 4,882 girls and women employed in the town's cotton trade compared to 2,821 boys and men.

21

Many men in the first half of the nineteenth century remained in handloom weaving, many in the handloom sheds. Others obtained employment in engineering or as labourers in the building trade. As handloom weaving declined and the demand for labour within the mills increased, more and more men entered the weaving mills though weaving still remained a strong bastion of female labour. In 1905 there were 8,005 male weavers in Blackburn compared to 16,604 females.[22]

The continued demand for female workers meant that in 1910 59% of all women over the age of ten worked, 78% of all unmarried women worked and 44% of all married women; the highest percentages in the country. Outside of cotton, some women worked in dressmaking, others in shops and laundries, whilst a few more were in domestic service. Cotton, however, was the dominant employer.[23] This also led to 'the textile unions (becoming) the pioneers of mixed unionism.'[24] In 1908, of the Blackburn Weavers Association's 17,000 members, 11,900 were women. Of the 1,862 members of the Card and Blowing Room Operatives Association, 1,489 were female. As will be seen in Chapter 5 such a high proportion of women may have been one reason for the lack of militant trade unionism in Blackburn compared to elsewhere.[25]

One result, however, of so many women employed in weaving was that although equal pay was the norm so also were low wages. Just before the First World War four-loom weavers, who were the industry's elite, received between 22s (£1.10) to 28s (£1.40) per week. This compared to 36s (£1.80p) to 40s (£2) for skilled men in the building trade during the summer months, 35s (£1.75) to 38s (£1.90) for skilled men in engineering and 35s (£1.75) to 43s (£2.15) for spinners who were predominantly male. In furnishing weekly wages were 34s (£1.70) and in printing 32s 6d (£1.62). Skilled weavers' wages only matched those of unskilled building labourers. Other workers within weaving received even less. Piecers, strippers, winders, warpers and three-loom weavers earned less than £1.[26]

The result of such low wages for men in weaving allied to the availability of relatively well-paid work for women had far-reaching results for many families in Blackburn. With both husband and wife in work, and perhaps some of their children, it was estimated that in 1905 some households had a weekly income of between £4 and £6.[27] As will be seen in later chapters, such a relatively high total income influenced leisure activities and housing in the town. But when a family was reduced to just one wage earner through age, unemployment, illness, accident or death then poverty could ensue. The need for more than one waged earner in a family often meant women working throughout their pregnancies and returning within days of giving birth. As will be seen later, this affected health and infant mortality.

Millgirls. The majority of Blackburn's weavers were women. Most were young single women but many were also married. It was quite normal for women to work up to the last stages of pregnancy and return to work soon after giving birth. This partly accounts for the high infant mortality rate that the town experienced. Many millgirls also had impaired hearing due to the constant noise. *Courtesy of Blackburn Museum*

Women earning a wage did little in Blackburn to bring about equality of the sexes. Though the male/female division may not have been so wide as in other communities, especially within the mill, it was still there. Even though women far outnumbered men in weaving it was not until 1911 that the first two women were elected onto the committee of the Blackburn Weavers Association.[28] But the inequality mainly showed itself in leisure pursuits, as will be seen in Chapter 7, and within the home. Women returned from the mill to a second day's work in the evening and a subservient role. It was even claimed that

> In Blackburn ... it is the usual thing for the husband, when he comes home late at night, to give his wife a kicking and beating. The women take it as part of the daily round and don't complain.[29]

Blackburn's cotton workforce also had a distinct age structure. Spinners had a working life of about twenty years which meant that very few remained beyond the age of forty. In weaving it was only slightly longer. In 1892 60% of the town's weavers were under 25 years of age.[30] When women eventually became too old to work they nearly all became full-time housewives whilst men on leaving often took on unskilled work or, if they had saved, became shopkeepers or publicans.

It was the gathering speed of work, coupled with poor working conditions, that kept the workforce young. About 80% of weavers had four looms under their control by the 1880s, and the machines were getting faster as technical improvements were continually made. Accidents also grew as faster looms meant a greater chance of losing an eye to a flying shuttle. Local opticians were renowned for their range of artificial eyes. But it was the practice of steaming that physically wore down the weavers the most. This was a form of artificial humidity, necessary to reduce breakages in the thread, which was created by injecting steam into the atmosphere through jets. This started in the 1860s, and by 1890 95% of Blackburn's mills used such a system. The water used was often contaminated, hardly conducive to good health, but the main debilitating effect on the workers was caused by the severe drop in temperature experienced on leaving work, for ventilation within the mills was restricted in order for steaming to work.[31]

One further aspect of the local economy that changed over the nineteenth century was the increasing size of the average mill. In 1860 30 had under 250 looms and 52 under 400. By 1895 the average weaving mill had 603, by 1912 the number had risen to 822. By that date only two mills remained with under 300 looms whilst 32 had over 1,000.[32] Compared to other Lancashire cotton towns, Blackburn had always had some of the largest mills. As far back as 1841 Blackburn had an average of 281 workers to a mill whilst Bolton had only 217, Bury 162 and Oldham 79.[33] As will be seen in the next chapter, amalgamation was the order of the day from the 1860s as the main cotton families bought up any mill that came onto the market. Many other mills merged through marriage. In this way industrial concerns grew larger with minimal extra building. But as a direct effect of the increase in size of cotton firms came a new managerial layer that intervened between the workforce and the millowner. As we shall see, this had important social and political consequences for Blackburn.

By 1914 not only had the size of mills altered but so had the cotton trade itself. The transport revolution in the guise of canals and railways helped this process greatly. The 127-mile long Leeds–Liverpool canal was a scheme to connect the river Mersey to the river Aire. This would complete a waterway connection from the Irish Sea to the North Sea. Work started at both ends in July 1770. It is perhaps again indicative of Blackburn's geographical isolation that it was the final town to be connected. The eastern section joining Rishton to Eanam was opened in 1810 and the final stretch from Wigan to Blackburn in 1816. After 46 years the canal age had finally linked Blackburn to markets both east and west.

The canal brought agricultural produce and coal to Blackburn as well as raw cotton. It took away cotton cloth. Its advantages over road transport were that it provided a far cheaper means of bulk transport than packhorses and carts could provide. Transport costs were cut dramatically which allowed cotton prices to fall, thereby increasing demand and encouraging further expansion both of the industry and the town.

The next major transport impetus for growth came with the arrival of the railways. The East Lancashire Railway Company, founded in 1843, was formed to build a railway line from Preston through Blackburn to Accrington, Burnley and Colne. The Preston to Blackburn section was ready by 1846, and thousands lined the track for its opening. The Blackburn to Accrington section opened in 1848 and the extension line to Burnley and Colne in 1850, with a connection from Accrington to Manchester. In the same year the Bolton, Blackburn, Clitheroe and West

The Leeds–Liverpool canal, started in 1770, was finally completed in 1816. The Blackburn to Wigan section was the last to be completed. Industry grew up along its banks as it stimulated trade. Some of the architectural shell of that industry remains. Appleby Corn Mill, shown as it was in c.1874, now houses the new Granada TV studios.

Courtesy of Blackburn Museum

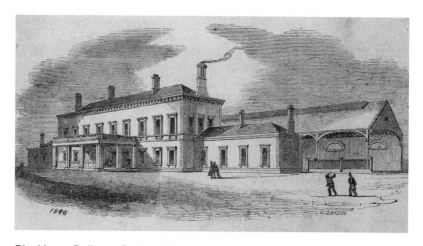

Blackburn Railway Station 1848. It remains little altered today. The East Lancashire Railway Company completed its Blackburn to Preston line in 1846 and thousands lined the track for its opening. The line to Accrington opened in 1848 and by 1850 Blackburn was connected by rail to Manchester. Just as industry was attracted to the banks of the canal in the early nineteenth century so now was industry to the railway since it gave a far quicker transport service. *Courtesy of Blackburn Library*

Yorkshire Co. opened a line between Blackburn and Bolton, extending this through to Yorkshire in the following years. By 1869 Blackburn was also connected by rail to Chorley, Wigan and St. Helens to the south west. Blackburn was now fully part of the national rail system. The cotton industry took full advantage of this and the mill building boom of 1849 to 1870 partnered railway growth.

The cotton trade had also altered in another way and this was its growing reliance on the export markets of the Far East. Even by the boom period of 1849–61 three-quarters of all the looms in Blackburn were producing cloth for the Indian market. By 1900 90% of all the town's cloth was exported to the Far East. But by 1914 India was beginning to manufacture her own plain coarse cloth which was Blackburn's staple product. Between 1905 and 1914 India doubled her loomage and increased her cloth production threefold.

Blackburn had come to her maturity by 1914 on the foundations of an industry which was nevertheless already in relative decline. Though cotton exports were still growing between 1890 and 1914, Britain's share of world consumption of raw cotton had fallen from 48.7% in 1870 to just 20% in

1913. Already foreign competition from Germany, U.S.A. and even India was squeezing Blackburn's products out of established markets. Blackburn's last cotton boom just prior to the First World War was in fact based on China as the town's millowners began desperately to seek out new markets.[34] But as Blackburn's Chamber of Commerce had warned in 1890, 'In Blackburn they had only one string to their bow ... they might some day deeply regret it'. The inter war years of the twentieth century saw this prediction come true. By then much of the town's character in terms of its physical shape, the habits of its people and the town's social and political structure had already been moulded by the cotton industry of the eighteenth and nineteenth centuries.

REFERENCES

1. *The Times*, September 1862, quoted in N. Longmate, *The Hungry Mills*, Temple Smith, London, 1978, pp.36–37.

2. P. A. Whittle, *Blackburn As It Is*, privately published, Preston, 1852, p.245.

3. G. Trodd, 'Political change and the working class in Blackburn and Burnley 1880–1914,' unpublished PhD thesis, University of Lancaster, 1974.

4. R. A. Light, 'The Lancashire power-loom breaking riots of 1826,' unpublished MA dissertation, University of Lancaster, 1982.

5. Trodd, 'Political Change'.

6. D. Walsh, 'Working-class development, control and new Conservatism: Blackburn 1820–1850,' unpublished MSc. dissertation, University of Salford, 1986.

7. *Manchester Guardian*, 4 December 1841.

8. For much that follows see J. G. Timmins, 'The decline of the handloom weavers in nineteenth-century Lancashire,' unpublished PhD thesis, University of Lancaster, 1990.

9. Walsh, 'Working-class development'.

10. D. Bythell, *The Handloom Weavers*, Cambridge University Press, Cambridge, 1969.

11. G. Trodd, 'The local elite of Blackburn and the response of the working class to its social control 1880–1890,' unpublished MA dissertation, University of Lancaster, 1974.

12. See printed census tables for 1881 and 1911.

13. Trodd, 'Political Change'.

14. *Blackburn Mail*, 12 April 1826.

15. G. C. Miller, *Blackburn: Evolution of a Cotton Town*, Blackburn Town Council, Blackburn, 1951.

16. For much that follows see M. Ellison, *Support For Secession: Lancashire and the American Civil War*, University of Chicago Press, Chicago & London, 1972.

17. *Blackburn Standard*, 4 December 1861.

18. *Blackburn Standard*, 17 June 1863 and 14 October 1863.

19. *Blackburn Patriot*, 5 October 1864.

20. *Blackburn Times*, 26 August 1893.

21. *Report of an Enquiry by the Board of Trade into working class rents, housing and retail prices together with the standard rates of wages prevailing in certain occupations in the principal industrial towns of the U.K.* Cd. 3864. (1908), cvii, p.319.

22. *Board of Trade Enquiry.*

23. Trodd, 'Political Change'.

24. S. Boston, *Women Workers and the Trade Union Movement*, London, 1980, quoted in E.M. Jones, 'Deference and the Blackburn Working Class: Operatives' Struggles 1852–1878', unpublished MA dissertation, University of Warwick, 1984.

25. Trodd, 'Political Change'.

26. *Board of Trade Enquiry*, p.91.

27. *Board of Trade Enquiry*, p.91.

28. Trodd, 'Political Change'.

29. J. Corin, *Mating, Marriage and the Status of Women*, London, 1910, p.128 quoted in Trodd, 'Political Change'.

30. Trodd, 'The local elite of Blackburn'.

31. Trodd, 'Political Change'.

32. Trodd, 'Political Change'.

33. *Report of the Factory Inspectors*, PP (1842), xxii.

34. Trodd, 'Political Change'.

3

Elites and political power
before 1914

Britain is a class society. That is not to say that society is static for class is fluid. The gradations of the British system have changed over time. In addition it has always been possible for individuals to climb up or tumble down the class ladder often taking their families with them. The period of the industrial revolution saw such changes.

The class structure altered to accommodate the rise of a manufacturing and professional middle class, the appearance of the wage-earning working classes and the later decline of the landed classes. During the hundred years up to 1850 class mobility accelerated. Then the portals of advancement narrowed as class stability re-asserted itself and fresh class barriers were erected. Concomitant with this change in the class structure came a change in the wielding of power. A new elite began to mould a new present and a new future. Blackburn was no exception to such change. In fact it saw the decline of the landed classes long before the 1880s from when most historians date their national decline.

The main pre-industrial power base in Blackburn as elsewhere was land, and the main seat of power the position of Lord of the Manor. From the early eighteenth century this position was not occupied in Blackburn by the aristocracy, and this was to have important consequences for the town. In 1721 Thomas Belasyse sold the Manor of Blackburn to William Baldwin, Henry Feilden and William Sudell. In the early nineteenth century the Feilden family bought out the other two.

The three Lords of the Manor were local and came from yeoman not aristocratic stock. Little is known of the Baldwin family after they were bought out, but both the Feildens and the Sudells moved into cotton where their real fortunes were made. Henry Sudell rose to become the greatest of the early Blackburn cotton merchants. Taking up residence just outside the town at Woodfold Hall, Mellor, he was reported to be a millionaire in 1820. But by 1827 he was bankrupt. Unwise foreign investments broke him, and he sold up and left Blackburn. Only the Feildens of Witton Park remained.

The Effigies of Thomas Belasise of Henknowle Baron L.d Lieutenant of the shire And one of y.e most Hon.ble the Right Hon.rbl Viscount Falconbergh Falconbergh of Yarum North rideing of York Lords of his Ma.ties Privy Councell &c.t

BONNE ET BELLE ASSEZ

R.White sculp.

Thomas Belasize (Belasyse) Viscount Falconbergh. His family were Lords of the Manor until 1721 when they sold it to William Baldwin, Henry Feilden and William Sudell, all of solid yeoman stock. This cut off Blackburn's links to the aristocracy, a severance that was to be influential in the future moulding of the culture of both the town and its people.

Courtesy of Blackburn Library

In 1880 the Feilden family still owned 2,000 acres throughout the Borough of Blackburn and drew rents from all parts of the town. Land still gave power even then, and many aspects of Blackburn's growth lay in the gift of the Feilden family. By intermittently disposing of parcels of land, generations of Feildens helped form not only the geographical pattern of the town but its civic, educational and cultural growth. Land was donated or sold by the family for, among many things, Corporation Park, the Technical College and the Grammar School.

By the mid nineteenth century most of the main members of this family no longer took an active part in the day to day running of their cotton mills. That was left to minor members of the family or even managers whilst they pursued other careers such as the military. They also had disappeared into the local political background by 1870. Though still very influential socially, occasional appearances on the local magistrates bench and on Tory platforms at election times now sufficed. Others had taken their place.

There were two main influences that explain the emergence and character of the middle-class elite that controlled Blackburn from c1850 up to 1914. The first was the success of the early cotton merchants of the eighteenth century who controlled the domestic system of manufacture. Some of these went on to become the early factory masters. In addition to the Feildens and the Sudells the main cotton merchants in the 1770s and 1780s were the Peels, Cardwells, Hornbys, Birleys, Chippendales, Maudes and Hindles.[1] Many were not originally Blackburn families but moved there to take advantage of the openings in the growing cotton trade.

The Cardwells, like the Lords of the Manor, were of yeoman origin. They came from the Preston area in the early eighteenth century, though it was Richard Cardwell, born in Blackburn in 1749, who founded the main family fortune. The Hornbys came from the Kirkham area on the Fylde. There they were local gentry. John Hornby, born in 1763, settled in Blackburn as a cotton merchant and went into partnership with Richard Birley, the son of a West India Merchant, also from the Kirkham area. The firm that they founded was later to build the Brookhouse cotton mills. The Peels too were originally yeoman farmers. They began in calico printing at Moorgate Fold in Livesey and at Church Brook.

It was mainly these merchants with a few newcomers such as the Glovers and Prymes who, having the capital and cotton connection, began Blackburn's factory system. By 1851 only the Hornbys and the Feildens still remained. Richard Birley's eldest son moved to mills in Manchester, all of Cardwell's sons made their careers outside of Blackburn, whilst the Peels, tired of having their spinning machines wrecked by locals, packed up and moved to Bury and Burton-on-Trent. Even in those families that stayed, the elder generation, having made their fortune, left Blackburn to enjoy their retirement in more congenial surroundings. John Hornby died at his seat at Raikes Hall near Blackpool. This is a pattern that persisted throughout the nineteenth century and, as will be seen later, may partly account for Blackburn's lack of major public buildings or high cultural heritage since those who made money from the town left to enjoy and spend it elsewhere.

The second influence to be noted is the relatively humble background of most of the leading families, another trait that was to be present up to 1914. With no local aristocracy to model themselves on, these families developed their own social mores more attuned to their new class position and often based on an idealised but modest country gentry. Again, as will be seen later, this had far-reaching effects on Blackburn's social, political, educational and cultural development.

Blackburn's first spinning mill was built at Wensley Fold in 1791 and others soon followed. In the late 1820s with the introduction of the power loom to Blackburn, weaving mills were added to the already established weaving sheds. The family names of Eccles, Haworth, Pilkington, Ward, Birtwistle, Livesey and Hopwood now enter Blackburn's history. Most of these men came from even more humble backgrounds. Richard Haworth was originally a draper in Northgate. William Eccles had lowly working-class origins, but rose to be a solicitor and thereby accumulated the capital to advance as an entrepreneur. Henry Ward, born in Mellor village in 1813, was the son of a barber. His father's business was far from large. 'So slender an income did it yield that it took Ward senior all his time to clothe and feed his family.' Henry too became a barber for a short while but with 'a bit of independent trading' by eighteen years of age had saved up the then tidy sum of £80 which he used to set himself up in the cotton trade.[2] William Birtwistle was brought up on a small farm near Great Harwood and raised his starting capital as a handloom weaver.[3] It was the fact that it was then possible in the early nineteenth century to enter the cotton business with only a modest amount of capital that allowed such men to rise so fast up the economic and social scale.

> The reason that little initial capital was needed was that many of the early mills could be leased or even rented. Many were not purpose built but were old warehouses. Yarn could be obtained on credit, worked up and sold before having to settle. In addition over half of those setting up in a new business began in partnership with one or more others. This meant that they only had to supply a part of the initial capital.[4]

This sum was raised in various ways. Many used the profits accumulated in some other business enterprise. Many cotton masters had been previously in business as shopkeepers, estate agents, builders or publicans. Others, like Henry Ward, raised capital away from their daytime occupation by acting as middle men and by doing some buying and selling on the side. Many even made their capital whilst working in the cotton industry. Having climbed the mill ladder up to manager, instead of a salary some chose to receive a share of the profits allowing themselves the chance of building up the capital to venture out on their own in an industry that they knew intimately. Other managers, because of the business acumen that they showed, were offered a partnership by their erstwhile employer.

By the second half of the nineteenth century this was far more difficult.

> Not so many years ago it was the ambition of half the minor traders, the shopkeeping classes of Lancashire, to get into the cotton trade. They assiduously saved up their profits until they had got a thousand pound, or perhaps two, when they at once proceeded to run up a weaving shed ... loom makers and machinists being quite ready to equip them with the plant, give them long credit and hoped for the ultimate payment of their accounts upon the profits that they might make.[5]

Increasing setting up costs stopped this happening anymore. In Blackburn, where the average size of mills had become larger, this had virtually ceased by 1860. At that date only 30 mills had under 250 looms and only 52 under 400. By 1895 the average weaving shed held 603 looms, a figure that rose to 822 by 1912. Thirty-two mills then held over 1,000 looms.[6] All this meant that even before the mill-building boom in Blackburn that just preceded the outbreak of the American Civil War, the day of the self-made factory master was all but over. Class mobility via the cotton industry was becoming rarer.

There was still the occasional exception. James Bead, who owned two mills in the 1880s, was the son of a spinner and had begun work himself in the Nova Scotia mills at the age of eleven and educated himself at evening classes. James Boothman, the son of a sailor, began as a weaver at one of Hopwood's mills in the 1850s. After working himself up to manager he bought his first mill in 1874.[7]

The millowning fraternity, however, was increasingly becoming a closed one and in order to keep it so was becoming increasingly interbred. By the last quarter of the nineteenth century 60% of the millowners in Blackburn had inherited their business from their father. Most others had succeeded into the business following marriage. Robert Hopwood Hutchinson's father had married the eldest daughter of Robert Hopwood. He inherited a fortune on his mother's death and, to keep the money in the family, used it to become a partner in Robert Hopwood and Son. By 1860 he was head of the firm and, as noted earlier, reputedly made £1,000,000 by running the cotton blockade during the American Civil War.[8]

Blood or marriage ties increasingly enjoined together Blackburn's new middle-class elite. William Coddington (MP for Blackburn 1880–1906) and Robert Hopwood Hutchinson were cousins. Joseph Dugdale, the main ironfounder in the town, and Michael Birtwistle, head of the Birtwistle group of cotton mills, were brothers-in-law. The millowners Henry Shaw and James Pilkington were also brothers-in-law, whilst the mills of James Bead and John Lund, were also linked by marriage.[9]

Another characteristic that this new elite had in common was that they were virtually all local men. In 1880 70% of them had been born in Blackburn itself while nearly all the remainder came from nearby villages. Very few outsiders had to be accommodated.

Once the millowning ranks began to close so also there was seen the erection of new class barriers to ensure that they remained the elite. The period saw the usual exodus of millowners who, having made their fortunes out of Blackburn, went elsewhere to enjoy it, but one consequence was the drawing up of a middle-class drawbridge. The 1870s saw the departure of the Pilkingtons, Jackson and Hopwood Hutchinson, but their mills were sold to already established local millowners not newcomers. This helped lead to the establishment of a narrowing plutocracy in Blackburn. 24% of Blackburn's leading late Victorian and Edwardian millowners left estates in excess of £100,000 at death compared to only 9% in the neighbouring weaving town of Burnley.[10]

But even within that elite there was a distinct pecking order. The Feilden and Hornby families led Blackburn's society. These two families were the sole survivors of Blackburn's cotton industry of the late eighteenth and early nineteenth century. Below them were the relative newcomers though they too by the second half of the nineteenth century were at least second generation middle class and some three.

The Thwaites were also a senior Blackburn family. Their Eanam brewery opened in 1797. But though Daniel Thwaites was the town's richest man at his death in 1888, he was always on the fringes of Blackburn's social and political elite. His attempts to enter the inner circle were continually frustrated by a Conservative caucus to which he never fully belonged. Money and pedigree were never enough on their own. The social mores of Blackburn's elite had also to be followed: mores based on an intermixing of an urban present with a rural past.

The dominant elite were a cross between urban employers and country squires. A lack of self-confidence in their new middle-class station, combined

Joseph Feilden. From the early nineteenth century the Feilden family were the sole Lords of the Manor. It was the way that this family either sold off or donated parcels of land that was partly responsible for the physical shape of present day Blackburn. *Courtesy of Blackburn Library*

with an affection for a pre-industrial past, led to a desire to claim roots that only existed in the imagination.

> When a Blackburn Master gets on he often develops into a 'swell' and though his father may have been a moulder, a blacksmith or a calico weaver, he talks about his ancestors, sends to the Herald's College for a crest and a coat of arms and buys an estate.[11]

Though this may have been an unkind exaggeration there is truth in it. The ceiling of Holy Trinity Church, painted in 1848 with the newly acquired coats of arms of all the Blackburn families who were the major subscribers to the building costs, is testimony to this. Such an imagined past also meant the need for this new elite to participate in, or give patronage to, such organisations as the Yeomanry or Artillery Volunteers and the Pendle Forest Hunt. This in turn moulded the way such disparate topics as law and order and leisure evolved in Blackburn, as will be seen in later chapters.

Most of the new elite also tended to live near each other in middle-class enclaves such as Preston New Road, out on the once exclusive high ground of the western suburbs of the town. Again, as the next chapter will show, this growing desire for class apartheid also helped mould the physical shape of Blackburn.

This new middle class also looked to give their children a separate education. At first the Nonconformists among them sent their sons to Hooles Academy, a commercial independent school, whilst many Anglicans sent their boys to Queen Elizabeth's Grammar School. As the public school movement reformed itself and expanded in the 1850s and 1860s many of these same families now packed their offspring away to boarding schools in Yorkshire, Cheshire, Manchester and Liverpool. The *crème de la crème* of Blackburn's elite were different again. This group sent their sons to the top public schools further south. Young Hornbys and Jacksons went to Harrow, the Briggs and Baynes to Rugby.

As Blackburn's elite moulded their new class structure and with it much of Blackburn, they also began to achieve their additional aim of taking control of the political reins of power. Their grasp as a class on Blackburn's representation at Westminster and on the town council was tightened, even when they fought out amongst themselves the secondary party political battle.

Blackburn had become a two-member Parliamentary Borough with the Great Reform Act of 1832. From the start the town's MPs came from the ruling elite and from the cotton industry. With only isolated, short-lived exceptions, such as Daniel Thwaites the brewer who was MP from 1875 to 1880, cotton dominated. Two families also dominated: the Feildens and the Hornbys. William Feilden became one of Blackburn's MPs in 1832 before retiring in 1847. His youngest son Montague Feilden followed in his father's footsteps in 1854. Joseph Feilden was MP from 1865 to 1869. His son Henry immediately took over what was virtually the family seat and held it until his death in 1875. The Hornby family began their parliamentary career in 1841 with the election of John Hornby, the fourth son of the original John Hornby who founded the Brookhouse mills. He was MP until

Laying of the foundation stone of the Cotton Exchange, 1863. The town's elite turned out in force and ensured that their presence would be recorded for posterity by commissioning a painting of the occasion. The painting now hangs in the town museum with the names faithfully recorded below. *Courtesy of Blackburn Museum*

1852. His elder brother William then replaced him in 1857, remaining in office until 1869 when he handed over what was then apparent family property to his second son Edward. He kept it until 1874. William's fourth son Harry recovered the seat for the family in 1886, retaining it until 1910. Between 1832 and 1910 the Hornby family had contested fourteen election contests and had only tasted defeat twice.

But whether the names of Blackburn's MPs were Feilden, Hornby, Pilkington, Briggs or Coddington their desire for political power was purely local not national. The Feildens never spoke in Parliament and Pilkington was similarly silent for the entire eighteen years that he sat in the House of Commons. Harry Hornby went even better, never uttering a single word from the backbenches in a twenty-three year career. Edward Hornby, in comparison, was garrulous. He spoke twice, which probably accounts for the fact that he never managed a second term of office. Blackburn could proudly boast 'if nothing more, that it has sent to the House as many, if not more, speechless members than any constituency in the country.'[12] What this emphasises is that becoming a Member of Parliament for Blackburn was merely a matter of achieving local status.

On the party political front it was the Conservative party that won control of the borough's parliamentary seats. The town became the 'Gibraltar of Toryism' in what was mainly Liberal Lancashire, especially after the 1867 Parliamentary Reform Act when the franchise was extended. The Liberals were represented by James Pilkington between 1847–65, but by the 1880s it had become a struggle for the Liberals to even squeeze in one member in a two-member seat. The last nineteenth century Liberal MP was William Briggs between 1874 and 1885. From then on a Conservative monopoly largely prevailed until 1914, broken only in 1906. The party's share of the vote shows the deep trouble the Liberal party found themselves in. In the 1880 election the Conservatives won 51% of the vote to the Liberals 49%. By 1892 it was 57% to 43%, then 73% to 27% in 1895. At the 'Khaki' election of 1900 the Liberals could not even field a candidate.

The struggle for power at council level followed a similar pattern. Blackburn became a municipal borough in 1851. The town was to have a mayor, twelve aldermen and 36 councillors. The borough was divided into six wards each with six councillors: St. Mary's, St. John's, Trinity, Park, St. Peter's and St. Paul's. Cotton dominated again from the beginning. Twenty-one of the 48 inaugural councillors and aldermen were textile manufacturers and two, classed as gentlemen, had a cotton background. Since the Charter of Incorporation stated that 'It is expected that men of business habits ... should be the men for municipal business', this surprised few. In the same way the first mayor of Blackburn could have been none other than a Feilden or a Hornby. It was in fact William Henry Hornby.

The number of aldermen with a cotton background had increased by 1881. At that date it was 79%. Amongst the openly elected council it was 41%. Though their position on the aldermanic bench held firm, by 1900 cotton's grip on councillors had declined to 17%. As cotton lost its firm grasp so did the middle-class elite. Their place was taken by shopkeepers and a rising professional class. They controlled 50% of council seats at the turn of the century. The remainder were held mainly by brewers, publicans, builders and other manufacturers.[13]

The cotton masters' grip on the local magistrates bench was firmer. By 1881 83% of the justices of the peace were millowners or gentlemen, a phrase used to describe mainly retired millowners or men who obtained their income from cotton investments. By 1900 this group still made up 62% of the total. Such proportions and higher can also be found on the School Board after the 1870 Education Act, the Burial Board and the Board of Guardians.

Growing dominance by the Conservative party of these same power bases can also be discerned. By 1880 25 of the 36 councillors were Conservatives. By 1889 it was 26. The aldermanic bench, being self-electing, was unswervingly Conservative. Together they gave a very comfortable majority with which to run the town. The School Board, the Burial Board and the Bench all had permanent Conservative majorities. On the Board of Guardians all except one of the 39 members were Conservative in 1895. Thirty-four still were at the turn of the century.

Conservative dominance was so great that the Liberals were prepared to give up the fight and come to pre-election agreements in order to retain at least a foothold. Council elections in many wards, therefore, were uncontested. On council committees Conservatives usually took the chair whilst Liberals were given the vice-chairs. As will be seen in the chapter on education, places on the School Board were shared out so precluding anything so democratic as an electoral contest. Relations were so amicable that the flag flying above Conservative headquarters even flew at half mast on the death of the Liberal James Beads in 1886. He, after all, was a cotton manufacturer and fellow member of Blackburn's elite. For the ruling class of the town both these factors came before party political loyalties in order of importance.

For the electorate, however, loyalty either to party or person largely explains the way that they voted, though that is not to dismiss other pressures. When Blackburn became a parliamentary borough in 1832 it had 637 registered voters. By 1852 this number had risen to 1,258. Prior to the Second Reform Act of 1867 the relatively small size of the electorate opened up the political process to various forms of influence. With majorities of only thirteen in 1832 and 1835 and of one in 1841, every vote counted in parliamentary elections. The consequence was a series of ways in which pressure could be brought to bear to maximise support and reduce opposition.

The electoral register was continually under scrutiny and attempts to have opponents' supporters removed on technicalities were commonplace. As the chapter on law and order will show, violence was a natural accompaniment to elections in Blackburn and much of that violence was politically organised. Exclusive dealing first made its appearance as early as 1832. This was pressure exerted by non-electors on those shopkeepers, tradesmen and publicans who could vote by threatening to withhold their trade unless they voted as told. Until the secret ballot was introduced in 1872 this could be highly effective. Non-electors could also have an important role to play on election day by just turning up in their thousands to make their feelings known, since those few who had the vote were obliged to cast it publicly.

Bribing and treating of the small electorate were also seen in the early years, helped by rich candidates and the prospect of close contests. The first election in 1832 saw beer barrels set up in St. Mary's churchyard. In 1852 treating was practised on such a wide scale that a parliamentary enquiry overturned the election result and forced a second ballot. The Liberal candidate, Eccles, had paid landlords who had previously voted Tory to set up Liberal committee rooms in their taverns and ply guests with free food and ale.

As the next chapter will show, many millowners were landlords to their workers. This could become yet another pressure point, especially after 1867 when many workers were given the vote for the first time. But it is also true that the political loyalty of those in non-employer-owned housing was virtually as committed to their employer's political stance.[14] In 1868 in the Walpole Street, Maudsley Street and Audley Range area of Park ward, where mills owned by Liberals predominated, voting was 52–22 in favour of the Liberal party. In Haslingden Road and Mosley Street, near mills owned by Conservative supporters, the voting was 144–51 in favour of the Tories. Employer-owned houses in these areas were few.

The 1867 Parliamentary Reform Act increased Blackburn's electorate from 1,845 to near 9,700, and this was followed five years later by the introduction of the secret ballot; thereafter many external pressures on voters declined though they were not fully eradicated. At the municipal elections of 1868 bribes were handed out quite openly under the guise of compensation for loss of earnings. These varied from 2/6d (12.5p) to several pounds. Complaints of 'bottling' or driving supporters of the opposing party out of town for the day were still being made in 1880. Claims that the age old inducements of free drink and meat pies were being liberally used were made in 1885.[15] Even in 1900 it was being claimed that 'it is notorious that the Blackburn Tory party wins its elections by means of the beer barrel'.[16]

In some areas the struggle even hotted up. Registration battles took on a new lease of life. The Revision court took a mere three hours in 1864 to judge on the eighty cases brought before it. In 1868 it took seven days to plough through 2,000 objections. These had originally been 6,000 but behind the scenes bargaining had at least reduced that figure. In 1873 4,000 objections had to be adjudicated and a further 2,000 in 1878.

The Conservative party were not loathe to use local levers to good effect to consolidate their dominant hold on Blackburn. They used the anti-Irish vote to good effect. Fuelled by both racial and religious hatred, the Home Rule in Ireland issue was often to the forefront of elections from the 1880s though the Irish question was never as important in Blackburn as it was in

Liverpool, Preston, Manchester or St. Helens where Irish immigration had been much more substantial. By 1901 Blackburn only had about 2,500 Irish-born residents, mainly concentrated in the Penny Street area. The Orange movement was quite strong, however, claiming 1,200 members in seventeen lodges and led by the brewers Thwaites and Rutherford and the cotton manufacturer Thompson.

Militant Anglicanism in varied forms also helped the Conservative party. The Conservatives were the party of the established church and the established church was dominant in Blackburn. In addition to the Orange Movement, Blackburn had a Church of England National Protection League with 900 members, and in 1885 a Church Defence League was formed. As will be seen in a later chapter, the Church of England fought hard for the control of the hearts and minds of Blackburn's population and was quite successful in warding off the spread of Nonconformism, the religious rock of Liberalism. Again as will be seen later, the way the Church of England won the battle to educate the borough's youth is yet further evidence of its power. Such influence could be transferred into political authority for the Conservative party.

The Conservatives also put up candidates who epitomised what Blackburn's electorate apparently looked for in their leaders. The people of Blackburn had a 'traditional dislike to strangers as their candidate'.[17] Between 1832 and 1859 not one 'stranger' won an election, and between 1865 and 1906 Sir Robert Peel in 1885 was the only exception and he had an historic connection. And local meant local. In the 1860s a certain J. G. Potter, a paper manufacturer from Darwen unsuccessfully stood three times. Although coming from a town virtually on the doorstep he was still seen as 'a stranger without any substantial interests in the borough'.[18] Blackburn had a very strong community sense bred in its self-inflicted isolation from neighbouring communities. Blackburn's people felt different to their neighbours and were proud of the fact. The actual birthplace of candidates was not of crucial importance. What counted was a strong stake in the community and an abiding interest in local affairs. The failure of John Morley, one of the most distinguished of Blackburn's parliamentary candidates and one who had been born in the borough, typifies this. On his return he was now seen as 'a London scribe'.

Harry Hornby, the town's MP for 23 years up to his retirement in 1910, typifies the kind of man that the people of Blackburn admired and looked up to. He was known locally as 'Mr. Harry', the 'owd 'un' or 'the gam' cock'. He personified the qualities most respected in Blackburn society. He had little knowledge of affairs outside the borough and had little interest in the evolving policies of his party. His outlook was basically apolitical yet when necessary he knew just what he stood for and stuck to his beliefs. Outside political change therefore merely washed over him. Harry Hornby remained a staunch believer in free trade even though eventually the majority in the Conservative party did not. Though a cotton man, the image he assiduously portrayed was that of a gentleman landowner and amateur politician. This image was roundly copied by Blackburn's elite. Hunting, horsebreeding, greyhound racing, coursing and cricket were far more important than politics. John Rutherford proudly kept a successful racehorse, whilst William Briggs, the only successful Liberal candidate in the late nineteenth century, gave humorous speeches in local dialect and constantly paraded his prize-winning greyhound on the election hustings. The abrupt shortness of Daniel Thwaites' political career was put down to his failure to match up to this image of 'Hornbyism'. Thwaites was too arrogant, too concerned in displaying his wealth and too aloof from local affairs to be seen as a 'real' gentleman.

The key to the success of Blackburn's elite, be they Conservative or Liberal, was that they won the respect, devotion and loyalty of Blackburn's working classes. Part of that loyalty was based on the fact that the town's workers accepted an hierarchical society. They did not ape the middle classes, merely admired them and dutifully accepted their place in the social order. Most loyalty, however, was based on the mill and was akin in many ways to present day loyalty to the local football team. Employers noted this and tended to stand for election in the ward in which their mills stood rather than the one in which they might live. As a contemporary observed in 1868:

> Each individual operative comes to identify with the mill at which he works, and if he be not troubled with convictions of his own readily accepts its political shibboleths.[19]

Political colours were sported at election time in the mills with workers even attaching them to their looms. When someone stood out against the rest, factory ejections took place and employers rarely had to become involved. Their employees did their work for them, often violently. The result of this tribal instinct was that streets loyally voted according to the political persuasion of the owner of the local mill.[20] Examples of this have already been given. Others are myriad. In Park ward, in the 1868 general election, the streets surrounding the mills of the Pilkington Brothers, Eli Heyworth and Briggs returned 626 votes for both Liberal candidates and only 312 for the two Conservatives. In the same ward in the streets encircling the mills of Harrison, Hopwood and James Thompson, all of whom were known Conservatives, only 212 voted for the Liberal candidates

Harry Hornby MP. Known locally as 'Mr. Harry', the 'owd 'un' or 'the gam' cock', he successfully carried on Blackburn MPs' tradition of silence by not speaking once at Westminster throughout his entire twenty-three year term of office that ended on his retirement in 1910. Though a staunch Conservative he had little interest in affairs outside the borough, a trait apparently much admired by the town's parochial electorate.

Courtesy of Blackburn Library

whilst 466 voted for the two Conservatives. And it was not just millworkers who loyally voted. In St. John's ward where Hornby's Brookhouse mills were situated, the landlords of all seventeen public houses voted Conservative as well as the owners of 20 of the 25 beershops.

Conservative party loyalty was also partly won within Blackburn by its leading adherents actively supporting issues that were close to the heart of the town's populace: issues such as factory reform and holding out against the introduction of the New Poor Law. This manipulation of working-class support is covered in detail in the chapter on social control and law and order. Blackburn's elite also won working-class loyalty and support through philanthropy and paternalism.

Back in the early 1800s, in times of hardship, Henry Sudell often provided vegetables at below market prices, and it was his annual custom to provide an ox for roasting in the market square at Christmas. The Pilkington's founded Blackburn Infirmary in 1858. Many of the elite financed the building of schools and subscribed to church building. In addition to building workers' housing, some also built public houses to serve them. Employers might forego rents in bad times and charge low rents in good. Hornby's even allowed old ex-employees to remain living in the houses rent free in the same manner as country gentry might look after old and faithful servants or tenants. During the cotton famine in the 1860s factory inspectors reported that half of the town's employers ran their mills on short time at a loss and also gave 'unobtrusive assistance' to their workers.[21] Turner provided almshouses and Eli Heywood provided a creche for nursing mothers as well as a canteen at his Audley mill.[22]

As a result, the hold that Blackburn's elite had on the electoral support of the people actually increased after 1867 with the addition of new voters. As the franchise was extended to encompass a growing number of the working classes the political dividend of their social control could be collected. The elite, and especially the Conservative elite, had cultivated and won the loyalty and support of the bulk of the populace. Blackburn's working classes had been well trained and now did their masters' bidding almost without question. As the nineteenth century wore on, however, and the Conservative elite saw off the challenge of their Liberal counterparts, a new threat did begin to emerge from below as a few members of the working class began to search for their own voice, whilst some even flirted with socialism.

Working-class movements had always been weak in Blackburn. As will be shown in a later chapter, though spontaneous and violent outbursts were relatively common, the working classes, in the intervening periods, were quiescent. Chartism was always weak, whilst other possible foci of working-class concern, such as the anti-poor law movement and factory reform, were successfully hijacked and manipulated by the town's employers. As will also be shown, trade unionism, though widespread, was conservative. Once the Standard List had been established in 1853, which gave agreed piece rates of pay for the job across all the mills in Blackburn, the concern of the unions was seen mainly as defending the status quo not actively pursuing radical change. By the last quarter of the last century, however, many local unions did feel it was time that they had a more powerful voice in local political debate. It was the textile unions who persuaded James Boothman to stand for Parliament in the General Election of 1885 under the auspices of the Labour Representation League. Their choice of candidate is telling. They picked a wealthy local cotton master. He came bottom of the poll.

The trade unions also resurrected the Trades Council. Originally formed in the 1860s, and a supporter of the Liberal Party in the 1868 elections, this first attempt at giving the unions a single voice soon disintegrated. It was resuscitated in 1884 to help in James Boothman's election campaign but had no permanent organisation until 1889. Even then, in the true spirit of Blackburn's working classes, it was far from being a radical organisation. The ruling body of the Trades Council was opposed to what it viewed as extreme politics, and in accordance with Lib/Lab tradition it expelled a member in 1896 for 'trying to force down the throats of the executive his own socialist ideals'.[23]

The fear of the Trades Council of what it saw as extreme political views was governed by the conservatism of Blackburn's trade unions. At this time the Blackburn branch of the Weavers' Association shunned socialism. It was worried about keeping its members. The Weavers' Protection Society, for example, was set up in 1885 as a breakaway organisation from the main union. By 1900 this group that openly supported the Conservative Party had 3,000 members. In addition the Conservative Working Men's Vigilance Committee was founded in the town in 1894 to fight radicalism in any form in the local trade union movement. The result was that in order to retain support Blackburn's trade union leaders had to tread warily in their search for a more vocal political voice. The success of Blackburn's middle classes in moulding a conservative workforce proved a formidable barrier in delaying any movement to the political left in the town's working-class organisations.

This is not to say that there were not attempts to form socialist and labour organisations in Blackburn. There were and some were even modestly successful. A local branch of the Social Democratic Federation was formed in 1884. This occurred soon after Henry Hyndman and

William Morris, the national leaders, came to speak in Blackburn during the weavers strike of 1883/4. By 1900 the town branch had one hundred members. These were not cotton workers, however, but mainly self-employed men such as shopkeepers, barbers and tailors. Their power base was therefore weak. And when compared to the membership of one thousand in neighbouring Burnley this socialist enclave is seen in an even truer perspective.

The weakness of socialism in Blackburn is also seen in the chequered history of the town's Fabian Society. A local branch was founded in March 1892. It was dissolved within a year, not to re-emerge until 1912. From its initial demise, however, arose a branch of the Independent Labour Party. But it too was never strong in membership terms. By 1903 it could only boast two hundred members. But at least it proved more successful in its longevity than most of its contemporaries. But perhaps the difficulties encountered by local socialists in converting the people of Blackburn to their political philosophy were summed up by a certain Tom Stephenson who explained that: 'It was very often the case of talking to a couple of men and a dog and a couple of kids'.[24]

After Boothman's dismal failure in the General Election of 1895 the next attempt to put up a candidate to represent explicitly the working classes of Blackburn was in 1900. A young Philip Snowden, later destined to become the first Labour Government's Chancellor of the Exchequer in 1924, stood as the Labour and Socialist candidate. This title was chosen specifically so as not to offend any single organisation. With no Liberal opposition, which allowed a straight run against the Conservative candidates, Snowden polled 25.5% of the vote totalling 7,096. It was not enough. In 1906, when again given an unopposed run at the Conservatives by the Liberals, Snowden succeeded. His 10,282 votes sent him to Westminster alongside the long standing Conservative MP Henry Hornby. The shock proved too much for Henry who never stood for Parliament again. But the result was not totally out of line with Blackburn's political past. With the Conservative Party horrendously split in 1906 over tariff reform, the wonder was that Blackburn still returned at least one Conservative MP. The constituency was one of the very few in the entire north west to do so.

It is interesting to note how Snowden chose to fight his election campaigns. He copied the tactics honed so successfully by generations of Hornbys and the remainder of Blackburn's elite. Policies took a back seat, as did the King's English. Snowden's successful 1906 election campaign poster cried out; 'We want a gam' cock that con feight. Snowden con. He's o'reight'. This was a fitting acknowledgement to the psychological hold that Blackburn's middle-class elite had on the minds of the workers of the town.

46

But Snowden's electoral success, however fleeting, cannot just be brushed aside. Cracks were beginning to appear in the working-class Toryism of Blackburn by the beginning of the twentieth century. It was being undermined as amalgamations and takeovers amongst the cotton mills, as noted in the previous chapter, increasingly diminished the number of cotton masters. Moreover, family firms were becoming limited public companies, and the growth of a deepening managerial layer in the enlarged firms and the rise of directors and shareholders led to a widening division between the workers and the remaining cotton kings. With their growing isolation, paternalism and the common touch grew weaker. As the elite's grip loosened, some workers, in the absence of a Liberal centre, crossed directly over to the left of politics. But as the political history of interwar Blackburn will show, this working-class Tory haemorrhage was not terminal. That it did not prove fatal is yet another tribute to the overwhelming success of the town's nineteenth-century elite in perfecting their stranglehold on Blackburn. Not only did they carve out for themselves their own dominant and influential niche in the town's social structure, with its own distinctive social mores based on an imagined semi-rural squirearchy, but they also won political dominance. In order to do this they successfully contrived to control, direct and mould the working classes of Blackburn with considerable success and lasting consequences.

REFERENCES

1. P. A. Whittle, *Blackburn as it is*, Privately published, Preston, 1852.
2. *Blackburn Times*, 26 August 1893.
3. *Blackburn Times*, 29 June 1889.
4. J. H. Fox, 'The social origins, careers and characteristics of entrepreneurs in South Lancashire during the 19th century', unpublished MA dissertation, University of Lancaster, 1970.
5. *Textile Mercury*, 3 September 1892.
6. G. Trodd, 'Political change and the working class in Blackburn and Burnley 1880–1914', unpublished PhD thesis, University of Lancaster, 1978.
7. G. Trodd, 'The local elite of Blackburn and the response of the working class to its social control 1880–1890', unpublished MA dissertation, University of Lancaster, 1974.
8. *Blackburn Times*, 26 June 1893.
9. Trodd, 'The local elite of Blackburn'.
10. Trodd, 'Political Change', table 10.
11. *Daily News*, December 1883, quoted in *Blackburn Standard*, 29 December 1883.
12. *Blackburn Times*, 16 September 1875.

13. Trodd, 'The local elite of Blackburn', p.14.

14. P.Joyce, *Work, Society and Politics*, Harvester Press, London, 1980, p.123.

15. *Blackburn Standard*, 3 April 1880, and *Blackburn Times*, 24 October 1885.

16. *Blackburn Labour Journal*, December 1900.

17. *Blackburn Times*, 18 September 1875.

18. *Blackburn Standard*, 24 March 1869.

19. W. Abrams, 'Social conditions and political prospects of the Lancashire workman', Fortnightly Review , October 1868, p.437.

20. P.Joyce, 'Popular Toryism in Lancashire 1860–1890', unpublished DPhil. thesis, University of Oxford, 1975.

21. Quoted in J.C.Lowe, 'Parliamentary Elections in Blackburn and the Blackburn Hundred 1865–1880', unpublished MLitt. thesis, University of Lancaster, 1970.

22. For full discussion of the paternalism of Blackburn's millowners see Joyce, *Work, Society and Politics*.

23. Quoted in Trodd, 'The local elite of Blackburn'.

24. Quoted in Stephen G.Jones, *Sport, Politics and the Working Class*, Manchester University Press, Manchester and New York, 1988, p.33.

4

Physical growth
to 1914

Between 1750 and 1914 Blackburn developed from a market town with less than 5,000 inhabitants with an expanding textile trade, to the weaving capital of the world with a population of over 130,000. Such an expansion obviously brought about great changes to the physical shape of the town. But urban development can be shaped by a variety of other factors. Among these are landownership, transport, industrial location, class divisions and civic intervention. It is the mix of such influences that determines the individual shape of each town.

Since Blackburn had partly developed as a market town serving its hinterland, the heart of the settlement in 1750 was centred around a crossroad where Darwen Street, King Street and Church Street met, near a crossing over the river Blakewater. From here it was possible to travel westwards to Preston via Feniscowles, Livesey and Witton or by an alternative route up Dukes Brow to Revidge then through Beardwood and Salmesbury; north east to Burnley and Colne through Whitebirk and Rishton; south east to Bury and Manchester via the ridge at Lower Darwen and along it to Eccleshill; north to Ribchester up Shire Brow and to Whalley via Wilpshire Moor and Whalley Nab.

Around this focal point centuries of gradual unplanned development had brought about a small conglomeration of twisting streets. A visitor described Blackburn quite succinctly in the 1790s: 'The town itself consists of several streets, irregularly laid out, but intermixed with good houses, the consequence of commercial wealth'.[1] A year after this description, the Reverend Thomas Starkie, the vicar of the Parish Church of St. Mary's, obtained permission to lease out the church's glebe land for building on a 999 year lease.[2] This land, totalling 70 acres and stretching for half a mile to the east of the parish church, previously used for farming or laying out bleached cloth to dry, soon became covered with mills, foundries, breweries and various workshops.

Cotton, however, was the spur behind Blackburn's accelerated development, and the shape of this industry's growth was always an important factor in the direction the town's expansion took. As we have seen, the last half of the eighteenth century was dominated by the cotton merchants who provided the spinners and handloom weavers with their raw materials and collected the woven cloth for sale and distribution. These merchants worked from warehouses mainly situated along King Street and Ainsworth Street.

In order to receive the raw cotton and then distribute the finished cloth these merchants needed a better road system. At the time many roads were often no better than rutted tracks. Those to Preston and Burnley were improved as early as 1754–55 whilst the route northwards into the Ribble Valley was improved when Whalley Road was turnpiked in 1776. To the east Haslingden Old Road was built between 1789 and 1791. Yet another turnpike trust in 1819–20 built Whalley New Road taking an easier, low route, whilst Preston New Road was constructed in 1825 reducing the distance from eleven miles to eight and half miles. Over the next two years Macadam, the great road builder, oversaw the building of Accrington Road and Revidge Road as part of a public work scheme to provide employment during the cotton slump of the time.

When the mills began to be built, since they needed water for production processes as well as to generate steam power, they were at first constructed along the banks of the river Blakewater, river Darwen and the Leeds–Liverpool canal. In 1867 35 mills and weaving sheds could be counted along the banks of the river Blakewater, 34 alongside the river Darwen and 39 by the side of the canal.

The great mill building boom of 1850–70 followed the advent of the railway age in Blackburn. This next stage in the transport revolution provided a far quicker and more efficient service stimulating yet further industrial development in the town. Mills were now free to move away from a waterside location, but since the railway chose roughly to follow the canal route through much of Blackburn this made little difference to industrial location.

But to visualise the shape of Blackburn's industrial growth as one of expanding ribbon development, stretching outwards along river and canal banks and finally by railway sidings, would be misleading. Though this did occur, it went hand in hand with the development of mill colonies. These were initially on the periphery of the town but subsequently developed in any remaining open space.

Three main ones coloured the development and shape of Blackburn: those at Brookhouse to the north of the town centre, at Nova Scotia to the south, and at Grimshaw Park to the south east. All began their life in the 1820s. The reason for their siting outside the town centre was partly that the land was cheaper and partly that buildings ripe for conversion and extension already existed there. These were old bleaching and dyeing works that had needed open spaces in which to lay out the cloth to dry. Both Robert Hopwood at Nova Scotia and John Hornby at Brookhouse took over such premises.[3] These mills needed workers and since, as will be seen below, most workers had to live within a few streets of their workplace, housing had to be provided next to the mills. Streets appeared and kept on appearing as the mills expanded and fresh ones joined them. As subsequent chapters will show, churches and schools followed, with the result that self-contained colonies grew up. By 1847 the colonies of Brookhouse, Nova Scotia and Grimshaw Park contained the largest mills in Blackburn which between them employed one third of all the cotton operatives in the town. By 1852 William Eccles alone employed 1,900 workers at his Nova Scotia mills.

Smaller colonies were continually being formed. In the 1850s the Daisyfield area grew up. Audley saw a rapid expansion between 1870 and 1900 around the mills of Eli Heywood, whilst at the same time the Mill Hill area developed between the railway and the canal around the Cardwell Mill of Mitchell Eccles and the Albert Mill of the Forrest Brothers. Yet another distinct area grew up around John Fish's Primrose Mill at Livesey and his Waterfall Mill alongside the railway on the Preston side of the town.

The result of such piecemeal development, centred around places of work, was that most of the working-class areas of Blackburn were a mixture of industrial and residential development. Higher Audley is a typical example. Mainly built in the late 1860s and early 1870s, the parish contained in 1906 a population of 7,722 living in 1,600 working-class dwellings in seventeen streets laid out in a grid iron pattern. Interspersed were five spinning mills, ten weaving sheds, two iron foundries and ten small workshops.[4] Such a pattern was repeated over and over again throughout Blackburn.

The housing within these colonies was partly built by the millowners themselves and partly by speculative builders. The building of homes for workers by millowners began at the first spinning mill in Blackburn at Wensley Fold. Early owners had built seven cottages by 1809, but by 1832 the new owners, Messrs Lund and Foster who had taken over the mill in 1816, owned 84 houses around the mill. By the same year Bannister Eccles and Co. had built 48 workers' cottages at their Darwen Street mills. By 1837 employers owned 270 such houses in Blackburn. Hornby owned 72 of them in five streets around his Brookhouse mill, constituting 70% of the housing stock there. By 1843 the number of workers' houses owned by employers had risen to 1,051 whilst by 1850 the figure had reached 1,588. Hornby-owned housing had now reached 185; 96% of the entire stock in the twelve streets surrounding his mills.[5] By the early 1870s employers

This aerial view of Blackburn, probably taken in the 1950s, serves to show how industry dominated the townscape and, thanks to the mill colonies, pervaded virtually all areas of the town. The walk from home to work was nearly always a short one, often just to the end of the street.

Courtesy of Blackburn Library

owned approximately 13% of the town's housing stock, though by the 1890s such property appears to have been largely sold off.[6]

The question still remaining, however, is why did the employer class build houses for their workers? Millowners providing homes for their operatives were not confined to Blackburn. It occurred in many textile towns in Lancashire and Yorkshire. For many it was an investment, but in most towns and cities such building declined in the 1840s when railway investment gave a far higher return on capital.[7] But in Blackburn it was precisely at this time that employer-owned housing accelerated. Another motive has to be searched for. Was it the continued need to house workers in a time of expansion? Because of the lack of local transport, workers had to live near their workplace, and much of Blackburn's industrial growth was taking place in mill colonies just outside the main built-up areas. Or could it be, as will be discussed in the following chapter, because of paternalistic attitudes adopted by many millowners? Alternatively, was it done in order to be able to influence or intimidate workers to gain social and political control over them? Perhaps the answer lies in a mixture of such motives. But for whatever reason these houses were built, many workers in Blackburn found that their landlord was also their employer.

The bulk of working-class homes, however, were built by speculative builders. These builders bought the leasehold of building plots off landowners. In Blackburn this was mainly off the church and the Feilden family, the Lords of the Manor, who, as noted in Chapter 3, owned most of the land in and around Blackburn especially after the bankruptcy of Henry Sudell in 1827. The leases were nearly all for 999 years. The builders financed themselves by the raising of short-term credit through mortgages negotiated through a local solicitor, insurance company or building society, usually the first. The mortgage would be repaid when the houses were built and sold. Most builders were small firms who built merely a handful of houses at a time, often just one or two. The purchasers of the completed houses were nearly always local people who were looking for a safe long-term investment for their capital, one on which they could keep a close eye. The bulk of such people owned less than ten houses each. They were small investors belonging to the lower middle class or even the prosperous working class. This 'shopocracy' looked for rents to bring a safe return on their hard-earned savings whilst their capital remained secure in the shape of bricks and mortar.[8]

Some building in Blackburn was done through building clubs. In 1822 the Blackburn Friendly Union for the building and purchasing of houses was formed and others followed. Members paid in an agreed sum per week. With this, land was purchased and building carried out. Often the order in which members took possession of their new house was decided by lot. Others raised mortgages from building societies or through local solicitors, but in Blackburn owner-occupation was limited. By 1914 it was still under 10% whilst in nearby Burnley, also famed for weaving and admittedly an exception due to the established and highly successful Burnley Building Society, owner occupation was estimated at between 33% and 50%.[9]

The 1850s saw the first main concentrated burst of housebuilding for the working classes in Blackburn. During the 1840s 1,433 houses were built. In 1851 alone over 1,000 new homes were constructed.[10] A map of 1852 shows new building taking place at St. Alban's, Brookhouse, Copy Nook, Cob Wall, Nova Scotia, Grimshaw Park, Bank Top, Witton, Daisyfield, Strawberry Bank, Limbrick, Shire Brow, New Branch Road, Eanam, Bridge Street and Salford. The main departure in this spurt of housebuilding was the expansion of working-class housing up the slopes of the surrounding hills. Those at

Strawberry Bank were seen at the time as model housing, 'airy, salubrious and well built, and delightful domiciles. They are a pleasant retreat from the busy hustle and bustle of the town for those who enjoy them.'[11]

Housing expansion was also seen after the end of the cotton famine in 1865. Between then and 1879, with the exception of a slight slump in 1874–76, an average of 400 new houses a year was built. In 1877–78 the total even reached 1,500. By 1879 Blackburn contained 19,042 houses compared to 6,648 in 1841 and 12,952 in 1865.

The typical working-class house built in the second half of the nineteenth century was terraced with four rooms. In the first ones built, the downstairs front room, opening directly onto the street, was the living room and kitchen and measured approximately 13ft x 14ft. The downstairs back room was generally used as a scullery and wash-house and measured about 10ft x 11ft. Between these rooms was a stairway leading to the two bedrooms which were exactly the same size as the two rooms below. The back door led to a yard which was paved or flagged and contained the lavatory, most of which were on the water carriage system using either waste or clean water, and the ashpit. This yard in turn opened onto a paved back street about 12ft wide.

From about 1890 an improved type of worker's house was often built, though it followed the same general arrangement of the previous one. In some the front room was now lobbied off and a scullery, with a slopstone and sometimes a washing boiler, was added onto the back room. This scullery was 6ft–7ft square. The back room was the kitchen and living room, the front room now becoming the parlour. In the front room was a drawing room grate whilst in the back room was a kitchen grate with an oven on one side and a hot water boiler on the other. There was a small unventilated pantry under the stairs. Upstairs a third bedroom and occasionally a bathroom were added. Of 20,000 working-class homes inspected in 1908, 16,000 were two-bedroomed and only 182 had bathrooms.[12] Very few back-to-back houses were ever built in Blackburn and where they were, mainly near the town centre, they had virtually all been demolished in improvement schemes by 1914. That working-class housing in Blackburn was of a higher quality than in many neighbouring towns was due to a local act of parliament passed in 1854 at the instigation of the new town council. This effectively banned back-to-back housing and set down minimum requirements regarding area, height and ventilation of rooms.

But where did the workers come from to fill these houses? Partly the population growth was due to the increased birthrate and even the decreasing deathrate that eventually characterised the nineteenth century. But Blackburn was also populated through migration from local villages.

This working-class property in the Salford area of the town, owned by the Thwaites family, was earmarked for demolition under a local Improvement Bill of 1879. The gentleman on the left is proudly standing outside the single seat privy that had to cater for the occupants of four houses. *Courtesy of Blackburn Library*

In the early years this migration was often forced. Millowners bought up cottages in nearby hamlets in times of depression and then evicted the weavers whilst offering them alternative employment in their Blackburn mills. As one local millowner explained to a government committee in 1838, 'villages from 2–6 miles distant were being depopulated, the inhabitants being encouraged by the manufacturers to be nearer the factories'.[13]

A study of migration into Blackburn between 1850 and 1870 has shown that it was mainly whole families that moved into town not just the young men and women, and that the average distance travelled was five miles per generation. Thus most of those who migrated into Blackburn came from nearby rural handloom-weaving settlements such as Mellor, Wilpshire, Pleasington and Tockholes. The reasons behind migration differed. They ranged from unemployment, the desire to increase family income whilst remaining in the same trade, which could mean the father sacrificing his own work in order for his children to find it, or to a change of trade perhaps to a shopkeeper or publican.[14]

Notwithstanding the constant population growth Blackburn does not seem to have suffered a housing shortage at any time during the nineteenth century. Admittedly in 1871 23% of all households contained at least one related member other than husband, wife or child, but that had more to do with the responsibilities of the extended family than a housing shortage. 23% of households also had lodgers, mainly single or widowed unskilled males, unmarried mothers and their children and a sprinkling of travelling salesmen.[15] This had more to do with tenants wanting extra income in order to pay the rent than a shortage of rented accommodation.

A housing shortage only appears to have hit Blackburn in the first years of the twentieth century when the numbers of houses being built annually often slipped into just double figures. The problem was not confined to Blackburn but was a national experience. The main reason was that the pool of small investors willing to put their savings into property in return for rental income was fast drying up. Rising building costs meant that in order to obtain a decent return on capital rents would have to rise to a level unaffordable by most tenants. In addition, with far more companies offering shares on the market both at home and abroad, attractive, alternative investment opportunities presented themselves. Whether such a change in investment habits by the 'shopocracy' was permanent or not is still debated by historians but no reversal had been seen by 1914.[16]

Perhaps partly because Blackburn never suffered a housing shortage until just before the First World War there appears to have been a high turnover of tenants in many houses. Between 1845 and 1851 in New Mill Street 9 of the 19 houses saw a change of tenant. In Old Mill Street 18 out of 28 houses saw such a change. In percentage terms this gave a 45% and 64% mobility rate. This compares to Union Street and Pump Street in the Nova Scotia area which saw movement rates of 66% and 57% over the same period.[17] Since some houses may have seen more than two tenants over this period the figures, if anything, depress the actual mobility rate of families.

This high tenant turnover in working-class areas does not seem to have diminished as the century wore on. Over 30 years later in a sample of 28 streets taken from the 1881 census covering 1,170 residents, only 47% were in the same house five years later and only 21.5% ten years later.[18] The reason for such high working-class mobility is probably because families moved on changing jobs to be nearer their place of work. Such job changes would be more frequent in a town such as Blackburn because of the relatively short working life of a cotton worker.

Henry Street photographed in 1958. Back in the 1820s this was a solidly respectable middle-class neighbourhood. As the nineteenth century progressed the middle class migrated to new properties built further away from the town centre and the mills. Henry Street was then taken over by the expanding working class in a 'filtering up' process.

Courtesy of Blackburn Library

Even the advent of the tram, the so-called 'gondola of the people', made little difference to workers' mobility rates.[19] Blackburn saw its first tram in 1881; its first corporation tram in 1886. At least two early morning and evening trams had to be provided for workers at the insistence of the town council but they were little used. In fact they were so little utilised that the tramway company asked for permission to withdraw them in 1891. They were still under-patronised in 1901. It is interesting to note that many of the termini of the tram routes – Witton, Billinge, Cherry Tree and Wilpshire – were all expanding middle-class suburban areas. It should also be noted that, except for encouraging suburban ribbon development, the tram had little effect on the spatial geography of Blackburn, only the visual. No new roads were built for trams, all extensions travelled along existing roads, and no roads were ever widened for the sake of the tram.

One other consequence of the nineteenth-century working-class habit of living within a few streets of the workplace was a lack of status division amongst workers. It is claimed that such distinctions were not as marked in Blackburn as they were elsewhere.

> Although the labourer did regard the craftsman as a little above him I don't think there is any hostility. They worked together, they lived together, they drank together in the pubs and their children married each other.[20]

This observation certainly seems to be borne out by the evidence. In 1871 in Moor Street, a run down working-class area near the canal, there lived nineteen skilled workers, 31 weavers and labourers and eight clerical workers and shopkeepers. In Cambridge Street, built relatively recently in the Audley area of town, 24 skilled workers, 33 weavers and labourers and four clerical workers and shopkeepers resided together.[21] Working-class residential divisions certainly appear to have been blurred.

The immigrant Irish population, however, were an exception.[22] Irish immigration to England was centuries old but the main influx started in the eighteenth century following the famine in the 1770s and Wolfe Tone's failed rebellion of 1798. In addition there was always the seasonal arrival of agricultural workers needed since the enclosure movement. A large scale influx began in the 1820s, but was mainly limited to Liverpool and Manchester. In 1841 only 9% of the Irish community in Lancashire was outside those two cities. This altered when Irish immigration accelerated after the great famine of the 1840s. In 1851 Blackburn had 2,505 Irish-born inhabitants, making up 2.8% of the population. By 1861 the figures were 6,378 and 5.3%. These figures actually underestimate the numbers in Blackburn's Irish community since they are based on registration districts and these take in many of the outlying villages that held few Irish. The figures also do not include any children born locally, and Irish families were frequently very large. The true figure for the town of Blackburn in 1861 is probably nearer 10%. The lack of skills of the majority of these immigrants and their readiness to accept low wages pushed them into menial jobs. The hostility of local, industrial, Protestant people, who despised these rural Catholics and looked upon them as an inferior race, led to their cultural and social isolation. Packed in ghettos made up of the oldest and poorest housing such as the Penny Street area, they formed their own clubs, public houses and friendly societies all under the watchful eye of the priest. As will be described later, these Irish communities often had to suffer violent incursions from their fellow townsfolk.

Blackburn's middle class were also socially distinct, but their segregation was entirely voluntary. At the beginning of the nineteenth century they

Woodfold Hall near Mellor. Once the home of Henry Sudell, Blackburn's first cotton millionaire, who went bankrupt in 1827. The property was then bought by the Thwaites family. Sudell set the trend for the richest of the town's middle-class elite to live as far away from the grime of the town as possible whilst remaining within easy daily travelling distance. The hall was safely surrounded by a nine-foot wall that stretched for four miles, keeping the great unwashed at an acceptable distance.

Courtesy of Blackburn Library

lived in large houses in the centre of the town, often with warehouses attached to the rear of their houses where those that were cotton merchants conducted their business. By the 1820s the middle class still lived in Georgian town houses on King Street and Clayton Street but they had also now spread out to St. Alban's Place and Montague Street. However, as the century progressed, and the fresh class barriers described in the previous chapter began to be erected, Blackburn's new Victorian middle class chose to live a still more exclusive and separate life from the working classes. The most illustrious of the merchants and millowners had already bought estates on the outskirts of the town and built themselves Georgian mansions. Henry Sudell lived at Woodfold House at Mellor. He surrounded his home with a nine-foot stone wall stretching four miles. After his bankruptcy, the Thwaites family purchased it. William Feilden built Feniscowles Hall complete with deer park, whilst Henry Feilden built Witton House. Those millowners slightly lower down the wealth league table contented themselves with building large houses though many of these were far away from their mills and sat in extensive grounds. William Eccles built one at Spring Mount

Ada Hopwood of the millowning Hopwood family in the drawing room of Holly Mount, West Park Road c.1900. This photograph gives an insight into the affluent though far from ostentatious living conditions of the town's elite. *Courtesy of Blackburn Museum*

which later became the Girls' High School. Those that built slightly later ensured their houses were more on the outskirts of Blackburn away from the encroaching dirt and grime. These included The Grange at Wilpshire, the home of one branch of the Pilkington family, and Pleasington Hall, built by the Hornbys in 60 acres of land in 1893.

The bulk of Blackburn's middle class though were not able to afford such houses but nevertheless lived well and lived together. This was mainly in the north west of the town where industrial development had not taken place, along Preston New Road and the roads leading off it up Billinge and Revidge hills. This higher ground was away from Blackburn's smells, smoke and working-class housing. The terms of their leases often prevented the building of public houses or industrial premises anywhere in the vicinity. From 1860 right up to 1914 this area set the social tone of the town. Of the 184 heads of household along Preston New Road in 1881, 113 were millowners, professional men or 'gentlemen'. The remainder were mainly high class tradesmen or widows with a private income. Little had changed by 1912 when 108 of the 191 heads of household were professional men,

This aerial view of Blackburn clearly shows the stark dividing line between the tightly packed terraced housing of the working class on the right and the more salubrious middle-class housing surrounding Corporation Park and along Preston New Road.

Courtesy of Blackburn Library

millowners or 'gentlemen'.[23] They also owned the overwhelming number of the few telephones in the borough. The typical middle-class villa was set back off the road with its own carriage drive and twelve to fifteen rooms, of which some were quarters for servants, usually two. Some villas contained a billiard room inside and had a lawn tennis court outside in the two-acre garden. As for the lower middle class, the clerks and travelling salesmen, many of these too lived in their own areas of the town such as Mill Hill. The dividing lines between this group and the working classes, however, were far fainter than they were between the lower middle class and the professional and employer class.

One other way in which Blackburn's wealthy middle class shaped the town's physical appearance was through the erection of public buildings, partly by philanthropy though mainly by voting through the sums required whilst sitting on the town's ruling bodies. A market house in early Italian palazzo style, with an interior measuring 186½ft x 109½ft, was erected in 1848 at a cost of £9,000. This stood at the end of King William Street on a spot formerly known as Sudell's Croft. It had a framework and roof supports entirely of iron with the roof divided into three spans supported by walls and two rows of iron columns, eight in each. Ornate decorations to the columns and ironwork were picked out and painted in bronze. There were eight arched doors, three at each end and one in each side. Over the central door a clock tower stood on four pillars with arches twelve feet wide. The whole building was illuminated by gaslight. It was claimed at the time to be unequalled in Lancashire. Four years later the new council, elected after incorporation, enlarged the market place by demolishing the property on the south side of the old market square. In 1870–72 a rather less awe-inspiring second market house, originally destined to be a fish market, was built.[24]

The newly incorporated councillors in 1852 also decided to build themselves a handsome new town hall in the Italian renaissance style. Erected next to the market it was finished in 1856 at a cost to the ratepayer of £35,000. Still looking to the Italian peninsular for architectural inspiration, the town's worthies spent ratepayers' money on a new court house and police station in King Street. Finished in 1872 the style of this municipal edifice was Venetian gothic. Blackburn Technical College was yet another public building to grace the town. Built at Blakey Moor in brick, the favoured style was high Victorian gothic. The foundation stone was laid in 1888 by the future King Edward VII when Prince of Wales.

What Blackburn still lacked, however, was a cotton exchange. Wednesday afternoons saw a weekly cotton yarn market at the Old Bull Inn. After incorporation in 1851 the council discussed building one on the site of the old market cross where Lloyds Bank now stands. Finally the millowners formed their own company to build one and a foundation stone was laid in 1860. It was originally envisaged as having two wings, one facing the town hall and one along King William Street. In the centre angle would be a tower. The timing was unfortunate, however, since the first half of this decade saw the cotton famine brought on by the blockade of the southern cotton-growing states during the American Civil War. The tower and the King William Street wing were built at a cost of around £9,000 in fourteenth-century gothic style containing an exchange room measuring 140ft. x 53ft. The second wing was never completed.

Perhaps the most imposing public building erected in the nineteenth century, in that it sat high above Blackburn in isolated, awesome splendour, brooding daily over the town's populace, was the workhouse. It was built

Original architect's design for Blackburn Cotton Exchange, 1863. The left wing was never built, thus allowing the Cotton Exchange to join the list of Blackburn public buildings that never quite matched the splendour of those in other northern industrial towns and cities. Today the heavily disguised main entrance admits you into a cinema whilst the only completed wing houses an Italian restaurant.

Courtesy of Blackburn Library

between 1861 and 1864 on the summit of a ridge to the south east of the town in 30 acres of land at a cost of £30,000. Though it was £5,000 cheaper than the town hall it was still designed to house 700 inmates.

By the end of the nineteenth century, thanks to the efforts of the council and the town's elite, Blackburn boasted a town hall, courthouse, market hall, technical college, workhouse and half a cotton exchange. All were connected with either the pursuit of money or social control. Other than in architectural style none had any connection with culture in the accepted sense.

The only exception was when a site for a library and museum was purchased by the council in 1871 and a building constructed in decorated gothic style. It fronted Richmond Terrace and France Street and cost £10,000. The sculpted exterior panels were paid for by local dignitaries but in size it pales into insignificance against those in other northern towns of comparable size. As for an art gallery, Blackburn is still waiting for one. A public hall in late renaissance style to seat 3,000 was planned just prior to the First World War on the same slum clearance site upon which the technical school was built. It was also to seat 1,000 in an assembly hall and 500 in a lecture hall. But Blackburn had to wait until 1921 before the complex was completed.

As one contemporary explained in 1852,

> Blackburn has been, perhaps justly, stigmatised by neighbouring towns as a place where the love of trade and pecuniary profit seems to have entirely absorbed every feeling for the enjoyment of the intellectual luxuries and ornaments of life; and the utter neglect which the fine arts have hitherto experienced, has been repeated in support of the allegations.[25]

The reason Blackburn's nineteenth-century elite failed to bring high culture to the town is probably because, as the previous chapter showed, they aped the narrow interests of an imagined squirearchy rather than the role of cultural patron associated with the aristocracy. For them to breed and own a prizewinning horse or greyhound was culture enough. Blackburn has suffered from this legacy ever since.

Blackburn's elite may have been uncultured, but at least they were practical men and this aspect of their character brought benefits to the town. The Improvement Commissioners, who came into being in the second quarter of the nineteenth century, began the task of making the town a better place in which to live. A local Act of Parliament for the better lighting of the town was passed in 1837 and a gas light company formed. Though in 1841 the local newspaper could complain of 'the bad state of the side-walks or footpaths, and in no town in England are they so rugged, so uneven and so irregular as in Blackburn ... the streets themselves (being) ill-paved, very irregular and entirely without crossings', they had to admit a year later that 'the inhabitants of Blackburn are beginning to experience the benefit of their Improvement Act in the many new footpaths which have been lately laid down and flagged'.[26]

But the main changes followed the merger in 1847 of the Police Commissioners, who had had responsibility for the upkeep and cleansing of the streets since 1803, with the new Improvement Commissioners appointed under a local Act of Parliament. This new body formulated a code of bye-laws, and then in 1854 its responsibilities were taken over by the new town council set up after incorporation in 1851. This council, which as we have seen in the previous chapter was mainly comprised of Blackburn's elite, began to exert throughout the remaining half of the

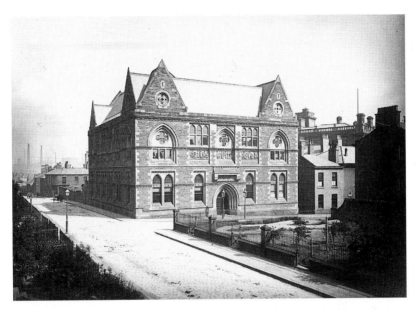

A photograph from about 1880 of Blackburn Free Library and Museum, facing Richmond Terrace and France Street, and built at a cost of £10,000 in 1871. The few sculpted exterior panels were each paid for by one of the local elite. Their philanthropy stopped there. This reflected their lack of interest in high culture and ensured a building far smaller than those in comparable neighbouring towns. *Courtesy of Blackburn Library*

nineteenth century a greater and greater influence over the daily lives of Blackburn's populace and the physical environment in which they lived. The influence the council had on the quality of the town's working-class housing has been noted. In 1878 the local gas supplies became municipally owned, followed by electricity in 1894 and all public transport in 1898. In 1882 the fire service, situated in Clayton Street and previously manned by volunteers, was taken under council control, and a new brigade formed from members of the town's police force. The council's input into law and order will be seen in detail in the following chapter.

One major way, however, that the town council affected the people's daily lives was in the area of public health. With the initial rapid urbanisation in the first half of the nineteenth century, devoid of building regulations and bye-laws, the general health of the town was poor, and Blackburn suffered regular outbreaks of infectious disease as well as more general ever present ill-health. Scarlet fever in 1811, cholera in 1832 and typhus in 1854 are but examples of repeated epidemics. In 1850 the rivers Blakewater and Darwen were

> a series of elongated cesspools (containing) all that is vile and putrid, throwing off poisonous exhalations, spreading the seeds of disease and death and even contaminating the very food of the living.[27]

To combat such evils as this, after incorporation in 1851, the new town council embarked on a number of measures. Some were entirely new whilst others began to build on the tentative start made by the Police and Improvement commissioners. Commencing in 1856 a public sewage system 30 miles in length was installed, complete with five settlement tanks, at a total cost of £100,000. At first the sewage outlet was on the banks of the river Blakewater at Wensley Fold. Then to stop such discharges into the river, a three mile culvert was built to the south west through Witton, Livesey and Pleasington to Hoghton Bottoms. Here a sewage farm was built. Then in 1875, as a result of Blackburn's continued expansion, 374 acres of land were bought at Salmesbury for £44,800 and an additional sewage farm constructed. A freshly cut culvert joined it to Hoghton Bottoms. To this improvement was added the power to convert all existing pail closet accommodation into water closets under the Blackburn Corporation Act 1901. Such pail closets numbered 10,000 in the mid nineteenth century and had never increased thanks to the tightening of building regulations following the 1854 local Act of Parliament. By 1914, despite all the new building, there were still only just over 9,000 pail closets in the town and the scene was set to eliminate them entirely.

As graveyards became full and yet another public health problem came to the fore, the town council set up a Blackburn Burial Board in 1854. Forty-five acres of land were purchased on the edge of the borough at Bank Hey in Little Harwood as a public cemetery. After it was walled and three mortuary chapels built, the total cost had reached £19,000. Opening in July 1857, it immediately averaged 2,500 burials a year, highlighting the earlier health problem of the disposal of the dead.

Refuse disposal was yet another problem of urbanisation. At the time of incorporation most refuse was merely thrown into the 20,000 ash pits or nearest water course, or piled on the nearest empty space. By the end of the nineteenth century the town council had provided four disposal plants and seven tips. The council also kept 60 horses to pull the town's refuse carts that now carried out collections. In 1908 the corporation obtained parliamentary powers to force local residents to provide galvanised iron dustbins, though this was not enforced until 1924.

The town obtained its first waterworks as early as 1772. Prior to that, ancient wells had sufficed. The original reservoir was sited in Pemberton Clough and was turned into ornamental lakes when the area was transformed into Corporation Park later in the nineteenth century. The Blackburn Waterwork Company was formed in 1844 to provide a more adequate supply for the town's growing population. New reservoirs were excavated at Guide and Pickup Bank on the outskirts of Blackburn. Water supply became municipally owned in 1875. Water supplies in the Bowland Forest area to the north of Blackburn were purchased and trunk mains built to carry the water to new storage reservoirs at Guide and above Corporation Park.

Such public health improvements increased life expectancy in Blackburn. This is not to say that the mortality rates in Blackburn were below the national average, but at least they were constantly falling. They were still above the national average in 1914 though they were better than those in Burnley which was the nearest equivalent weaving town. In Blackburn, Burnley and England and Wales respectively the death rate per 1,000 people was 21.3, 21.6 and 19.5 in the 1880s. By 1914 the corresponding figures were 15.0, 16.3, and 13.8.[28]

Death rates also varied greatly throughout nineteenth-century Blackburn for they were class-based. This was still the case at the beginning of the twentieth century even after so many public health improvements had been made.[29] Between 1900 and 1909 the average middle-class death rate in the town was seventeen per 1,000. It was 24.6 in St. Mary's Ward which was a central working-class district. It even reached over 40 in some canalside slum areas. Meanwhile in St. Silas ward in the middle-class Preston New Road area the rate was only 12.8.

Infant mortality was also at its greatest in the central working-class areas of Blackburn. Poverty caused by low wages rather than poor physical conditions appears to have been to blame. The Medical Officer of Health put down the high infant mortality rate in certain areas to the undernourishment of pregnant women, to the fact that many worked right up to the last stages of pregnancy, and to the poor feeding of babies on dinner scraps and contaminated milk. A survey of 10,000 Blackburn children in 1911 reported that 94% of them showed some signs of undernourishment whilst 16% were actually malnourished; 30% of the pupils at St Gabriel's School were diagnosed as having rickets caused by a deficiency of vitamin D.[30]

Life for most in Blackburn by 1914 was still hard. The town had developed into an industrial community dominated by mills and endless streets of terraced housing. Just a few public buildings stood conspicuously in the centre of the town. The employing and professional middle class had mainly formed their own enclave on the higher ground to the north west whilst the majority of the working classes clustered on the lower land, perhaps looking worriedly over their shoulder to the workhouse on the ridge opposite. A canal and a railway line now joined the river in bisecting the town and tram lines criss-crossed its main streets. The town's shape had been set for good or ill, and it was the town's elite, in their dual role of employers and civic leaders, who had been the main influencing factor.

REFERENCES

1. J. Aiken, *A Description of the Country from 30–40 miles around Manchester*, London, 1795.
2. *Blackburn Mail*, 20 April 1796.
3. J. D. Marshall, 'Colonisation as a factor in the planting of towns in North-West England', in H. J. Dyos (ed.), *The Study of Urban History*, Edward Arnold, London, 1968, p.228.
4. St. Matthew's Church centenary booklet, Blackburn Library Local History collection.
5. D. Walsh, 'Working-class development, control and new conservatism: Blackburn 1820–1850', unpublished MA dissertation, University of Salford, 1986.
6. P. Joyce, *Work, Society and Politics*, Harvester Press, London, 1980.
7. A. Howe, *The Cotton Masters 1830–1860*, Clarendon Press, Oxford, 1984.
8. D. R. Beattie, 'The origins, implementation and legacy of the Addison Housing Act 1919, with special reference to Lancashire', unpublished PhD thesis, University of Lancaster, 1986, chapter 2.
9. G. Trodd, 'Political change and the working class in Blackburn and Burnley 1880–1914', unpublished PhD thesis, University of Lancaster 1978.
10. P. A. Whittle, *Blackburn as it is*, Privately published, Preston, 1852.
11. Whittle, *Blackburn as it is*.
12. A. Greenwood, *Report on the Housing of the Working Classes in Blackburn 1908*, in Blackburn Library Local History Collection.
13. Bannister Eccles to 'Enquiry into the conditions prevailing in the northern districts', quoted in Walsh, 'Working-class development'.
14. J. C. Doherty, 'Short-distance migration in mid-Victorian Lancashire: Blackburn and Bolton 1851–1871', unpublished PhD thesis, University of Lancaster, 1985, pp.333–353.
15. Trodd, 'Political change'.
16. Beattie, 'Addison Housing Act', Chapter 2.
17. Walsh, 'Working-class development'.
18. Trodd, 'Political change'.
19. J. Clay, 'The Tramways of Blackburn 1851–1949', unpublished BA dissertation, Lancashire Polytechnic, 1984.

20. A worker in Blackburn Calico Printing Works, quoted in Trodd, 'Political change'.

21. Trodd, 'Political change'.

22. What follows is mainly based on A. Granath, 'The Irish in mid-nineteenth century Lancashire', unpublished MA dissertation, University of Lancaster, 1975.

23. Trodd, 'Political change'.

24. W. A. Abram, *A History of Blackburn Parish*, J. G. & J. Toulmin, Blackburn, 1877.

25. Whittle, *Blackburn as it is*, p.ix.

26. *Blackburn Standard*, 12 May 1841 and 10 August 1842.

27. J. Withers, 'A report upon the sanitary condition of the Borough of Blackburn 1853', Blackburn Library Local History Collection.

28. Memorandum in support of application for constituting the County Borough of Blackburn a City, undated (1934?), in author's possession.

29. Blackburn Centenary Souvenir, Blackburn Town Council, Blackburn, 1951.

30. Extracted from the annual reports of the Medical Officer of Health and the Annual report of Blackburn's School Medical Officer 1911.

5

Law and order, popular protest
and crime 1750–1914

In a small isolated community everyone not only knows everyone else but usually knows everyone else's business. As a consequence when anything illegal occurs suspicion is often quickly narrowed down, even if the 'culprits' are not always betrayed by the community to those in authority. For those within such a community it is difficult to commit a crime and remain undetected. In such enclosed, pre-industrial societies the common types of crime would also reflect the prevailing economic and social structure. A high incidence of poaching, for example, would be found in rural areas. The forces of law and order would similarly evolve to combat this; gamekeepers in country districts, excise men in coastal areas and a civil watch system in towns. Industrialisation, which brought about not only a rise of population but a concentration of that population, meant radical and rapid economic and social change. This in turn led to changing criminal habits. The growth of industrial towns and cities with wage-earning workforces also gave rein to new forms of popular protest. In turn the forces of law and order had to undergo Darwinian evolution to combat such change.

The original, medieval seat of government in Blackburn was the Lord of the Manor. His grip on law and order was exercised through two courts: the Court Baron and the Court Leet. The former was a private court in which the Lord of the Manor upheld his own rights and privileges over his tenants and in addition settled disputes between those same tenants. The Court Leet was a public court obtained by royal grant. Here men and women could be punished by fine and imprisonment for such crimes as drunkenness and theft. From the time of Cromwell's Commonwealth the functions of this latter court in Blackburn were taken over by the Select Vestry. This group of prominent citizens, that always included the vicar and his curate, annually elected a parish constable who had to be a freeholder of the parish. He also had to be a man of some substance because the post became only honorary. The man elected hired a deputy constable to carry out the actual work. The position of deputy constable was only a part-time

71

post and was limited to looking after the town during daylight hours. A good deputy constable might well be kept on by a new parish constable so that some continuity existed. In addition a regular watch was instituted in 1794 to cover the hours of darkness.

As urbanisation then speeded up, systems of law and order more quickly evolved. In 1803, following a local Act of Parliament, the Police Commissioners took over the responsibility of appointing the parish constable, in addition to their other duties that included seeing to the upkeep and cleansing of the streets. Almost immediately the commissioners decided on change. From 1805 it was decided that Blackburn would have a full-time, paid, parish constable. The post was given to the then deputy constable, a butcher named John Kay. He was to remain in office for 25 years. John Kay was also given two full-time deputies. The nightwatch was formally disbanded in 1827. It had been revealed as an inadequate anachronism: the two workmen employed in 1825 were found in a drunken stupor whilst on duty. The responsibilities of the watch were given instead to the new constable and his deputies. They were helped for a while by a bellman who alerted citizens to such matters as lost children.

Urban expansion and the still faster growth of population necessitated further strengthening of the forces of law and order. In 1839, after the Police Act was passed at Westminster, a county police force was established in Lancashire and a branch took up residence in 1841 in King Street. The parish constables now passed into history. A superintendent, a Mr. E. Shepherd, was in charge and under him were four sergeants and twenty constables: one for every 1,440 inhabitants. Ten years later, as soon as Blackburn was incorporated as a borough, the town's elite immediately formed the borough's own police force in 1852 with a Mr. Laverty as its first chief constable. This was mainly done in order to replace the county force with one over which the ratepayers of the town had greater control, especially over the annual cost of law keeping which, it was claimed, had increased eight fold with the coming of the county force in 1841.[1] This borough force took over a building further down King Street backing on to Clayton Street. It had one superintendent, one sergeant and ten constables. Dressed at first in tall beaver hats, long-tailed blue coats and white trousers, they were armed with a truncheon and equipped with a rattle until whistles were introduced later in the century. The force totalled 35 by 1863, 89 by 1879 and 112 by 1885. This gave a ratio that had risen to one policeman to every 1,000 inhabitants.

It is interesting to note the backgrounds of these men. Though records only exist for appointments after 1889 there is no reason to suppose that recruitment patterns had changed dramatically from what they had been twenty to thirty years earlier. About two thirds of new constables were local. Their average age on recruitment was mid twenties and approximately half of them were married. Considering that Blackburn was a cotton town, it is worth noting that less than one third of the recruits had such a background, though this rose to one half of the local men. The remainder tended to be unskilled labourers or carters, interspersed with a sprinkling of tradesmen such as butchers, joiners, plumbers and tailors. One third also had some form of military experience, mainly those from outside the area. All were Lancashire men who presumably applied to various forces in their home county on leaving the colours.[2] Women did not enter the borough police force until 1947. In fact Blackburn was one of the very last forces in the country to appoint them. A town Conservative in politics also spawned a conservative police force.

As this local force grew prior to 1914 so did their premises. From King Street they moved to the rear of the newly-built town hall and then in 1913 to a purpose-built station in Northgate. In the meantime decentralisation had taken place as the population and the town grew. Under the command

Duckworth Street section of Blackburn Borough Police Force. Blackburn's force was almost entirely comprised of local or at least Lancashire men. Very few, however, had a cotton background. Over half of the recruits had previous military experience in the army or navy, making them used to discipline and the obeying of orders. The remainder mainly came from the ranks of tradesmen or labourers.   *Courtesy of Blackburn Library*

of sergeants, outstations were opened, firstly at Copy Nook to cover that and the Brookhouse area. Others soon followed such as at Revidge and Livesey. Local police now patrolled their local area. The force also expanded in other ways to cope with the new problems that urbanisation brought. A part-time mounted section of nine men, seven being ex-cavalrymen, was recruited in 1892. By 1912 there were thirteen, though they were still part-time.

Just as the police force grew in tune with population growth and urbanisation so did the court system. At the beginning of the nineteenth century there were no Blackburn magistrates. Normally prisoners had to be taken before magistrates in Preston, Burnley or Whalley.[3] If, on occasions, a magistrate had to travel to Blackburn, courts were held in the parlours of various inns or later in the town's Assembly Rooms. By 1852 a Sessions House had been opened in King Street, and Blackburn also had by then twelve magistrates of its own. The court continued to move to larger and more suitable premises until it finally settled in its present home in Northgate in 1913.

As for imprisonment in the late eighteenth century, the original lockup was a cellar in a small building used by the local watch that stood by the stone bridge over the Blakewater in Darwen Street. As more room began to be required the cellars of public houses began to be rented, as and when needed. The problem was finally solved when the first police stations were opened. Blackburn never had a prison. Convicted criminals were either sent to hulks at Deptford on the Thames or to Preston prison which opened in 1789. Those charged with the most serious offences were often held there or at Lancaster whilst awaiting the Assizes.

Law and order in the eighteenth and nineteenth centuries were initially not just in the hands of the emergent police force. One reason for their growth, and the creation, for example, of mounted forces, was the fact that they slowly took over public order responsibilities from the army. At times of public unrest, such as in the early nineteenth century, troops of cavalry and companies of infantry had often been billeted in the town.[4] At one stage they were deemed so necessary for the preservation of law and order that pressure was exerted to build a local barracks so that an armed presence would permanently be available in Blackburn. In 1829 the major inhabitants of the town, the bulk of whom were the millowners, wanted a barracks built on church land near the canal backing on to Bolton Road.[5] Pressure for a barracks holding up to 800 men was still being applied in 1838.

Though the main property owners were unsuccessful in bringing the army permanently to Blackburn, they were successful in keeping law and order under their control. This was crucial if they were to ensure social, political and economic stability. The Select Vestry, which had responsibility for law and order until 1803 and which numbered anything from nine to 24 members at any given time, was the preserve of the main freeholders of the town. They ensured that the annually appointed parish constable was of their own class and standing. When the Police Commissioners took over in 1803 and the borough council in 1851, the name of the controlling body may have changed but the membership did not. As the nineteenth century progressed the main landowners, industrialists and merchants kept strict control of the reins of law and order. An analysis of fifty of Blackburn's elite in the last quarter of the century shows that forty of them were Justices of the Peace at some point in their careers.[6]

Their grip on law and order appeared necessary. As people came together in towns like Blackburn, for the first time in large numbers, they began to realise that they could wield a collective voice. The seductive power of that voice, allied to action in the form of demonstrations, strikes and even riots, began to encompass many issues. To the middle class these activities seemed to threaten the status quo. This status quo was not necessarily sacrosanct, but if it was to be altered then it had to be guided in a way that the new urban ruling class approved. Their hold on the forces of law and order would help to ensure this.

Early stirrings of community action were seen during the Napoleonic Wars. The shortage of food brought about by the dislocation of trade and especially the high price of corn was the cause. In 1800, when the price of wheat rose to 118s 3d (£5.91) a quarter, attacks were made on farmers in order to seize their produce. The Riot Act had to be read. The middle classes of the town mustered in the form of the cavalry and infantry of Blackburn's Loyal Local Association of Volunteers. Officered by members of the Sudell, Birley, Feilden, Cardwell and Hornby families this 'who's who' of Blackburn's elite galloped to restore order.

Again, in 1808 a crowd attacked provision shops in Darwen street. Four ringleaders soon found themselves arrested, tried and convicted. Over fifty years later in 1862, during the hunger brought about by the cotton famine caused by the American Civil War, Blackburn's populace tried to rescue four men convicted of poaching in order to feed their families. Keepers and police were jostled and then stoned. As they retreated to the Town Hall for safety the crowd followed, smashing its windows. They then proceeded to do the same along Northgate, down King Street, up Montague Street and finally along Preston New Road. Again the Riot Act was read, and two hundred special constables were sworn in. A troop of the 5th Lancers was also sent for. Prison sentences of up to three years were meted out as the town's ruling class showed both their control and their displeasure.

Robert Parkinson in dual role as Mayor of Blackburn and as Captain in the 4th East Lancashire Rifle Volunteers, 1875. The elite not only controlled industry in Blackburn but municipal government and local law

and order. The latter was through the magistrate's bench and the local militia which the elite officered and which was called out to aid the police force in times of unrest.   *Courtesy of Blackburn Library*

If extreme class animosity was to show then the area of industrial relations would expose it. Blackburn's elite would in turn have to demonstrate that they were able to manage any such outburst if they were to consolidate their social control. The first riots that industrial Blackburn witnessed were industrially motivated, when in 1768 handloom weavers from Darwen, Mellor, Tockholes and Oswaldtwistle met up in town with local spinners. Their successful aim was to destroy the cottage of James Hargreaves, who had invented the spinning jenny, and Peel's Mill at Brookside, which had installed them. Machine-breaking riots broke out again in 1779 during a trade depression. All forms of machines were the target this time, carding machines as well as jennies. Only jennies with less than twenty spindles were spared. It has been suggested that many of the merchant 'putters out', fearing that those mechanising could undercut their prices, encouraged the rioters in their destruction and that magistrates even protected rioters from punishment.[7] Machine-breaking, it appears, was to be allowed if it were felt to be in the interests of the majority of the local elite.

The early years of the nineteenth century, though ones of hardship brought about by the Napoleonic Wars' disruption of trade, were actually ones of relative industrial calm. Following wage cuts amongst weavers in 1800 a few food riots broke out, but the fresh spate of machine-breaking of 1812, labelled as luddism after their mythical leader Ned Ludd, never came nearer than Bolton. 1818 saw the largest action. Up to 4,000 cotton workers paraded through Blackburn with a tricolour at their head. But their object was not political, and when they reached the home of the main employer Henry Sudell of Mellor, the timely granting of a 5% wage increase soon peacefully dispersed them.

Trade union activity did grow, however, over this period. Twenty-four workers' combinations were based on local inns in 1794. Due to the anti-combination laws of 1799 and 1800 they were forced underground under the guise of friendly societies. When the Golden Ball Inn on Blakeley Moor was demolished in the early twentieth century a secret room was found. This, it is believed, was a relic of illegal trade union activity. Soon after the Napoleonic Wars ended, the new disguise was a mushrooming of scientific and botanical societies which again met at various inns.[8]

1826 saw the next and last major outburst of machine breaking. It came amidst high unemployment. By April of that year 14,000 out of a population of 26,000 were receiving poor relief in some form or other and the number was increasing daily. This coincided with the late introduction of the power loom to Blackburn's mills. Bannister Eccles & Co. were the first to install them at their Dandy Mill in 1825. Others quickly followed. Add to this concoction the worsening plight of the handloom weavers and a heady

Fish Lane (now Cardwell Place) 1854 – the birthplace of the first Sir Robert Peel. The Peel family were forced to flee Blackburn at the end of the eighteenth century after rioting spinners destroyed the spinning jennies that they had installed in their mill. They took their business to nearby Bury.   *Courtesy of Blackburn Library*

brew was ready to spill over. In 1826, of the 10,686 local weavers, 6,412 were unemployed and a further 1,467 only worked part-time. On top of this wages were being cut.

> The very real evil about Blackburn ... is the number of weavers who, having become small manufacturers .., (are) obliged to sell at any price they can obtain and to make up their losses by reducing the wages of their weavers.[9]

The power loom therefore was a convenient target on which to wreak their frustration.

Small outbreaks of violence began to occur in March 1826 when the home of the Clerk to the Justices of the Peace was attacked and then the coaches taking the millowners to and from Manchester were stoned. As a result of this forewarning, when the main outbreak of violence occurred in

Volunteers on parade on Alexandra Meadows, May 25th 1863. Most of the elite were members of local volunteer militia units that were called out on a number of occasions during the nineteenth century to support either the regular army or the local police in putting down disturbances after the Riot Act had been read. In this way Blackburn's middle-class elite helped protect its hard won social, economic and political position from unruly elements from below.   *Courtesy of Blackburn Museum*

late April, the forces of law and order were ready.[10] Starting on Enfield Moor where the roads from Blackburn, Burnley, Whalley, Clitheroe, Haslingden and Accrington converged, five hundred weavers gathered, armed with home-made pikes, sledgehammers and a few guns. After an orgy of machine-breaking at Accrington, Wood Nook and Rough Hey they descended on Blackburn around midday. By now their ranks had swollen to around 6,000. The first troop of dragoons that attempted to halt them were swept aside and the 212 power looms in Dandy Mill off Darwen Street wrecked. Although the Riot Act had by now been read, the mob split up to search out more power looms and the military began to open fire. By evening the crowd on the streets had reached 10,000 and all the power looms in Blackburn had been destroyed.

.This day of violence was deceptive, however. Other than the power looms nothing else was touched. Other property including spinning machines was respected and hurt to individuals avoided. Even the millowners and the military held back as much as possible. Despite all the

Clayton Grange, Wilpshire, gutted by fire during the riots of May 1878. The rioters were venting their wrath on Colonel Robert Raynsford Jackson who was leading the employers' side in the negotiations during the cotton strike of that year. He and his family escaped by minutes. The rioters did not and retribution soon followed in the form of up to fifteen years' imprisonment. This escapade was an isolated militant aberration on behalf of a usually quiescent Victorian Blackburn working class.

Courtesy of Blackburn Library

mayhem and the shooting, casualties could be counted on the fingers of one hand. When the crowd was finally dispersed the dragoons only used the flats of their swords. The aftermath was also a relatively low key affair. Only 42 rioters were sentenced in the courts. Although ten were initially sentenced to death, commuted later to transportation, the rest were only imprisoned for between six to fifteen months. One reason why the millowners did not stamp down harder was that they realised that this was not an attack on themselves by the new working class but a dying spasm of the old. The employers' confidence in the future was shown by the fact that by 1830 the mills of Hopwood, Hornby, Eccles, Turner, Howarth, Feilden, Briggs and Rodgett had all installed fresh power looms employing 3,500 power loom operatives.

From this time organised trade unionism actively began exerting its influence, although mainly a conservative one. Blackburn's power loom

Jug commemorating the riots of May 1878. One side depicts the burning of Colonel Robert Raynsford Jackson's home in Wilpshire whilst the other shows the second day of unrest when a mob rampaged along Preston New Road breaking the windows of the houses of the town's middle classes. Since such working-class unrest was rare compared to neighbouring towns, this jug was made to commemorate the event. Though the jug illustrates the riot itself it really records the successful crushing of it, and the tight control of the lower classes, by Blackburn's middle-class elite. *Photo by Ian Beesley courtesy of Blackburn Museum*

weavers were unionised in 1840 and from the start they tended to concentrate only on industrial issues. Their first major strike at Hopwood's Nova Scotia Mill in 1847 fizzled out when arbitrators found their wages fair and reasonable. Though strikes were not rare, it was not until 1878 that intense, violent industrial trouble disturbed Blackburn's millowners again.

A 10% cut in wages in that year brought out weavers all over North-East Lancashire, 20,000 in Blackburn alone. The strike reached its height in this town on 11th/12th May. When news reached Blackburn that talks in Manchester had broken down many workers lost patience. The chairman of the employers' side was a local man, Colonel Robert Raynsford Jackson who lived at Clayton Manor in Wilpshire on the outskirts of the town. After

BLACKBURN RIOTS, MAY 1878.

gathering on Blakeley Moor a crowd of 5,000 decided to march on Col. Jackson's house, attacking a number of mills on the way in addition to the Hornby home. Clayton Manor was burnt to the ground though the family managed to escape by minutes. Martial law was proclaimed and 12th May saw 120 cavalry, 250 infantry and 800 special constables disperse a crowd on the rampage through the middle-class Preston New Road district. The law came down hard. Two received sentences of fifteen years, one of ten years, three of seven years and one of five years. Many others received lesser prison terms. A month after the riot the strike was lost.

But 1878 was an aberration and an aberration that was successfully confined. Blackburn, compared to its neighbours, was one of the most peaceful of weaving towns right up to 1914. The ability of the town's millowners in knowing just when to bend to circumstance helped bring this about. The introduction of the 'standard list' in 1853 typified the employing class's ability to control their workers by meeting them part way. The 'list' established an agreed rate of pay for a piece of work throughout all the mills in Blackburn. Since wage rates were the primary issue for the unions, disagreement was reduced to a minimum and industrial peace maintained at its maximum. The skill of Blackburn's millowning elite in manipulating the support of the working classes and channelling their energies down less destructive and dangerous paths can also be discerned in other areas.

Factory reform was one. A Short Time Committee was formed by millworkers in 1825 to press for the eleven-hour working day. At first it failed to get off the ground, but was re-constituted in 1836. But now the town's employers began to take control of it. The Factory Act of 1833 that limited the working hours of children was welcomed and supported by Blackburn's majority Tory millowners. Hornby, Briggs, Feilden and Townley claimed in the local press that they were the only ones trying to keep to the spirit of the Act. Though a way of attacking the Whig Government, this tactic also allowed them to hijack the leadership of the factory reform movement in Blackburn. Richard Oastler, on his visit to the town in 1836, may have told his audience how to ruin textile machinery with a stocking needle if millowners failed to enforce the factory acts, but his advice was not needed. Such action was pre-empted by the majority of factory masters taking up the cause themselves. They even called for a ten-hour working day and supported the abolition of the Corn Laws.[11] In this latter cause the millowners treated 1,200 demonstrators to tea at the James Street school in 1845.[12] The millowners led, whilst the workers followed.

The middle classes even ensured that the Poor Law worked as humanely as possible. Before the 1834 Poor Law Amendment Act, outdoor relief was the norm in Blackburn, with the average number in the workhouse only being 250 and these mainly being the old. By the time the new act came into force in the town in 1838 the Select Vestry members, the magistrates and the Overseers of the Poor had all been at pains to show how little would change. The result was little outcry when the New Poor Law took effect. This was also helped by the fact that the main organised opposition to the new law were the Operatives Conservative Association, patronised by many leading millowners including W.H. Hornby. Eleven of the twelve newly appointed Guardians were major employers or professionals, the remaining one being a shopkeeper. These Guardians were even criticised by the Commissioners in London for being too lenient towards the poor, and they were told to reduce both the 'luxuries' in the workhouse and the amount of outdoor relief.[13] By ignoring these instructions and by publicly coming out against other iniquities of the poor law, such as the splitting up of husband and wife in the workhouse, the middle-class elite obtained the support of the labouring classes and ensured that anti-poor law agitation was significantly absent in Blackburn compared to other parts of the north west.

A different way of keeping order and maintaining social control was shown in 1827. In this year the Vicar and Churchwardens decided to levy an extra ley-rate to pay for new heating and lighting in the parish church. This caused an outcry. Placards appeared all over the town calling on the people of Blackburn to fight a tax from a pre-industrial age that other towns had rid themselves of. Led by a spinner, Edward Hammond, a mass protest meeting, held in the parish church itself, turned rowdy. The result was prayer cushions torn, hymn books ripped and pews damaged. Finally the vocal strength of the demonstrators forced the church to allow a vote on the imposition of the extra rate. Public meetings were then held on Blakeley Moor, handbills, broadsheets and pamphlets printed. On polling day a mass picket was staged. Many voters found themselves 'jostled by them to the great injury to their apparel'. By a majority, the vote agreed that the ley rate should be levied, but a lesson had been learned. Never again did the churchwardens try to raise one.[14] It was time to bend with the wind of change not to stand against it. In this way control could still be maintained. Similarly 1862 saw nearly 400 working-class men hold a meeting in Blackburn market place to demand an end to the labour test asked by the Poor law Guardians before they would grant poor relief. They succeeded. Again the Guardians knew when to bend.

The success of the employer class in leading and directing many working-class movements, rather than trying to oppose them or even just standing aloof, is graphically seen in the funeral processions of prominent millowners. It was not uncommon to see hundreds of workers walking behind the funeral cortege whilst thousands of others lined the streets. Though class divisions did exist and at times led to conflict, Blackburn's relative quiescence compared to most other north-west towns was remarkable.

One other change that Blackburn's elite had to beware of, overcome or control was the growing political awareness, interest and participation that came hand in hand with urban growth. Only four men in Blackburn were arrested for political offences between the outbreak of the French Revolution in 1789 and 1803, a much lower number than in other north-west towns.[15] But starting from this handful of radicals wanting political change around the turn of the nineteenth century, meetings of up to 2,000 were seen in 1831 demanding parliamentary reform prior to the 1832 Reform Act. Again, in the lead up to the 1867 Reform Act, parades were held calling for an extension to the franchise. In the meantime elections grew into violent affairs. Violence occurred in five out of the nine elections held between 1832 and 1859 and twice the military had to be called in from Preston. During the 1830s and 1840s public participation usually took the form of spontaneous general rioting, when shops, public houses and committee rooms were wrecked. In 1842, after an investigation into the 1841 election decided to allow the result to stand, the Bull Inn, used by the Conservatives, was attacked. The Riot Act had to be read and the 60th Rifles called in to restore order.[16]

Perhaps the main expression nationally of working-class consciousness in the nineteenth century was the Chartist movement that erupted in 1838/9, peaked in 1842 and then raised its head for the final time in 1848. In 1838 and 1839 meetings were held in Blackburn, causing the vicar of the parish church to publish a sermon against Chartism which was bound and presented to the Queen. But despite the vicar's fears, the response of the people of Blackburn was 'somewhat apathetic' according to the Chartists themselves.[17] Certainly the call for a general strike in August 1839 passed off peacefully unlike in nearby Bolton. The historian Duncan Bythell claims that this was because the employment opportunities at this time were better in Blackburn than in the surrounding districts.[18] If Chartism was a 'knife and fork' issue, then the workers of Blackburn apparently had a full enough plate.

1842 was a different matter. Mass meetings were being held as early as March at which Richard Marsden, a local Chartist leader, called for militant action. In August a regional meeting was held in Bolton to which Blackburn delegates went. They brought back with them on Sunday 14th a decision to strike in order to force the government to grant the Charter. Stoppages started in many Blackburn mills the next day. Meanwhile, strikers from Stalybridge and Manchester, who had come out on the 8th and had then proceeded to march on neighbouring towns to turn out the workers, arrived in Blackburn. Newly sworn in special constables and the 72nd Highlanders awaited them. Mill after mill was attacked, some successfully, others not, as police used their cutlasses and the soldiers their muskets. When peace was restored one woman was dead. The strike lasted a further three weeks before crumbling. Of the rioters eleven were transported to Tasmania and 58 received prison sentences.[19] The millowners, when under pressure, had used their control of the forces of law and order to crush discontent and deter further expression.

As a result, Chartism virtually died out in Blackburn. 1848 merely saw an attempt to set up a co-operative venture based on Feargus O'Connor's land plan. The Operatives Sick and Burial Club purchased a small plot of land towards Pleasington on which a dozen families settled. It failed after three years.[20]

Despite the violence of 1842, Chartism in Blackburn never reached the heights it did elsewhere. One reason may be because the mills in the town were the largest in the north west at the time with an average of 281 workers per mill.[21] This allowed, as we have seen, paternalism and mill loyalty to develop. As the *Blackburn Standard* boasted in 1839 after a regional Chartist meeting:

> Blackburn, to its lasting honour, be it said, contributed very little either to the strength, interest or importance of the day's proceedings .... Indeed it may with truth be said that in few towns of its size and

importance in the manufacturing districts are to be found in a greater degree the elements of pacific organisation or where the spirit of industry – the co-operative discharge of social duties – are more strongly valued.[22]

Political violence carried on in the 1850s and 1860s but curiously this time it was organised by the town's elite. Unchecked working-class intervention in the political process was recognised as a dangerous threat by the middle-class ruling elite of Blackburn. They therefore decided to use and manipulate such violent energy for their own ends. Millowners on each side began to recruit 'bludgeon men' to break up rival political meetings and to defend their own. This led to fierce street battles, vicious running fights and attacks on rival public houses that supplied free beer to supporters. In 1853 several public houses that supported the Liberal cause at Bank Top and Whalley Banks were nearly gutted. In 1868 local Conservatives hired 6,000 bludgeon men as against 3,000 Liberal men. The result was that it was claimed that Liberals could not reach the polling booths 'without extreme personal danger'. The Riot Act had to be read and the police and military called out. With clubs, 'picking' sticks, hammers, bricks and paving stones all being used, 'the cracking of heads sounded like so much crockery being broken'.[23] The lesson learned by the middle classes was that if violence to further political aims was inevitable then it was better to lead and channel that violence and in such a way as to further their own ends.

The relative quiescence of Blackburn's working classes, except when called onto the streets to do the bidding of their 'betters', left the police in Blackburn generally free to concentrate on crime. Prior to 1861 the documentary evidence on crime is minimal and scattered. Highwaymen were reported in 1793, pickpockets apparently descended in droves from Manchester on fair days, and body snatching hit the headlines in 1827 when two men were surprised removing the corpse of a recently drowned woman from the graveyard of the Independent Chapel. The major crime, however, in the late eighteenth and early nineteenth century, if the food riots or machine-breaking rampages are ignored, was at least a non-violent one. It was moutre-snatching, the embezzlement by handloom weavers of the cotton thread left by the putters-out.

From the mid nineteenth century, crime statistics are more forthcoming though still fragmentary.[24] Serious crime was relatively small. Between 1851 and 1885 there was an annual average of one murder, two manslaughters and one rape. Muggings over the period fell from just under 30 per year to under ten. Robberies from shops and houses totalled an average of just under 200 per annum. Prostitution was a problem. The number of known prostitutes rose from 96 in 1855 to 127 in 1861. A peak was reached during the cotton famine years and then recorded numbers fell back to 48 by 1880. Total reported annual crimes throughout the 1870s averaged 4,450. Victorian Blackburn was not a law-abiding town when considered alongside the average of only five hundred reported crimes per annum during the 1930s. The nineteenth-century figures were matched, however, by the 1960s when the total once again passed 4,000: 4,112 in 1968.

A large percentage of the nineteenth-century crime figures were arrests for drunkenness and other drink-related offences. Back in 1835 the Vicar of Blackburn's description of the town's working class alluded to the problem of drink.

> Their immorality in every respect, their gross, filthy habits, their ruffian-like brutality beggar all description. The sabbath breaking and drunkenness are dreadful. The beer shops have increased the latter to a frightful extent.[25]

The view that drink increased crime was supported by the chaplain of Preston prison.

> There is a greater proportion of the uneducated classes in Blackburn than in Preston and the passion for liquor is a source of ruin and disgrace, more fruitful than any other source combined.[26]

Drink certainly was a problem. The number of drunkenness cases brought before the magistrates after 1862 rose steadily from approximately 400 to over 1,000 reached in the years 1876,1877,1881 and 1885 though figures thereafter gradually fell back.

But much of the crime prior to 1914 appears to have been caused by poverty and a sense of hopelessness rather than drink. This can be seen in that most recorded offences were committed by the lower working classes. In 1879 the Irish, who lived in the poorest areas of the town and did most of the menial and unskilled labouring jobs, made up 28% of all men arrested and 34% of all arrested women. Of the 1,986 people arrested in 1881, ten years after Forster's Education Act, 837 were illiterate, 1,120 could only 'read and write imperfectly', leaving only 29 who were fully literate. This is another indication that most crime, or at least most arrests, was limited to those at the bottom of society. In addition Blackburn had a large floating population. 1861 saw 107,675 registrations in the 36 registered lodging houses. The Chief Constable of the time ascribed much of the crime committed in the town to these men on the tramp.

It is interesting to note, however, that crime against property prior to 1914, which could be interpreted as a crime against the economic and social system, was minimal. This is yet further evidence that Blackburn's ruling middle-classes successfully kept control of class dissension. There had been sporadic outbreaks of working-class militancy but for the bulk of the time, especially after 1826, these outbursts were either guided by Blackburn's employer class or short-lived. Comparing their experiences with those in neighbouring towns, Blackburn's elite could stand proudly at the head of their workforce. How much pride the workforce could muster is another matter.

REFERENCES

1. Colin Hey, 'A History of the Police in the County Borough of Blackburn', unpublished work in Blackburn Library Local History Collection.
2. Personnel records of Blackburn Borough Police Force 1889–1907, Blackburn Library Local History Collection.
3. *Blackburn Mail*, 7 August 1808.
4. e.g. *Blackburn Mail*, 14 September 1808 and 6 February 1828.
5. Letter to Vicar of Blackburn 13 May 1829 quoted in G.C. Miller, *Blackburn: Evolution of a Cotton Town*, Blackburn Town Council, Blackburn, 1951.
6. G. Trodd, 'The local elite of Blackburn and the response of the working class to its social control 1880–1900', unpublished MA dissertation, University of Lancaster, 1974, Appendix 1.
7. W.A. Abram, *A History of Blackburn Parish*, J.G. & J. Toulmin, Blackburn, 1877.
8. 'Brief History of working-class movements in Blackburn', unpublished and unattributed manuscript in Blackburn Library Local History Collection.
9. Major Eckersley, military commander in Manchester 16 April 1826, PRO. H.O.40 19/1, quoted in R.A. Light, 'The Lancashire power-loom breaking riots of 1826', unpublished MA dissertation, University of Lancaster, 1982.
10. See Light, 'Power-loom breaking riots' and Abram, *History of Blackburn Parish* for the story of these riots.
11. *Blackburn Gazette*, 26 June 1839.
12. Quoted in W. Durham, *History of Blackburn A.D.317–1868*, T. H. C. L. Books, Blackburn, 1988 reprint.
13. See D. Walsh, 'Working-class development, control and new Conservatism: Blackburn 1820–1850', unpublished MSc. dissertation, University of Salford, 1986; D. Gadian, 'A comparative study of popular movements in north west industrial towns 1830–1850', unpublished PhD thesis, University of Lancaster, 1976.
14. *Blackburn Mail*, 12 September 1827 and 26 September 1827.
15. Alan Booth, 'Reform, repression and revolution: radicalism and loyalism in the north west of England 1789–1807', unpublished PhD thesis, University of Lancaster, 1979.

16. *Blackburn Standard*, 4 May 1842.

17. *Northern Star*, 30 March 1839, quoted in Duncan Bythell, *The Handloom Weavers*, Cambridge University Press, Cambridge, 1969.

18. Bythell, *Handloom Weavers*.

19. Walsh, 'Working-class development'.

20. Walsh, 'Working-class development'.

21. Gadian, 'Popular movements in North West'.

22. *Blackburn Standard*, 10 July 1839.

23. *Blackburn Times*, 7 November 1868.

24. Chief Constable's reports to the Watch committee 1861–1879, and Criminal and statistical returns of the Blackburn Borough Police 1881–1885.

25. Rev. John Whittaker's report of Blackburn to the Bishop of Chester 1835, quoted in Miller, *Evolution of a Cotton Town*, pp.28–9.

26. Annual report of the chaplain of Preston Goal, 1833, quoted in Miller, *Evolution of a Cotton Town*.

6

Education
1750–1914

Before the industrialisation process began to affect Blackburn the educational opportunities for its inhabitants were limited. For the most part, only the very rich and the very poor were catered for. Like many other towns Blackburn had its own small boys grammar school, founded in 1514, clinging tenaciously to life and providing a bare modicum of learning for its few fee-paying pupils from comfortable middle-class backgrounds. At the other end of the spectrum came establishments like the Girls Charity School founded in 1763 to enable ninety chosen daughters of the poor to be 'clothed and educated in knitting and sewing, reading, writing and arithmetic'.[1] Even the workhouse system had its attendant school. But for the bulk of Blackburn's children who fell between these two extremes there was little provision. This was slowly to change in the nineteenth century when schoolbuilding was spearheaded by the religious bodies, especially the Church of England, and by the town's elite, with cotton manufacturers to the forefront. Often they worked in tandem. Their motives, however, were not always purely educational in the sense of instilling into the young the basics of the three R's.

Though educational opportunities for most of the children of Blackburn in the late eighteenth and early nineteenth century were limited, there was a scattering of Dame schools and other private establishments. Dame schools, as the name suggests, were mainly run by women though sometimes men. Often these people took up the occupation because they were unable to do any other work or sometimes because it provided a much needed second income. The main attraction of these schools was that they were cheap and they formed a child-minding service in an area where female labour was needed either in the mills or in the domestic system. The standard and breadth of teaching varied widely but for many families that was of secondary importance. Such schools saw their heyday at the beginning of the nineteenth century.[2]

Private schools also originated in the eighteenth century but carried on expanding as the Dame schools declined. In 1839 there were 39 such schools in Blackburn, the vast majority day schools. They were small, averaging only 29 pupils in each establishment.[3] The reason for their growth was the emergence of an expanded middle class in Blackburn and of a shopocracy. Such people saw the value and need of an education and could afford it. These schools also catered for the education of middle-class girls. Whilst sons could go to the grammar school or one of the commercial academies discussed below, daughters needed an educational outlet. Many of these schools provided just that, taking such girls from the ages of seven to seventeen. A newspaper advertisement placed by a Miss Clayton described a school in Penny street for 'the education of a few young ladies' in writing, arithmetic, plain, fancy and ornamental needlework, drawing, dancing, music, French and geography. The cost was 25 guineas per annum for boarders and four guineas for day scholars.[4]

The number of these private schools eventually fell when demand from the lower middle classes and shopocracy declined following the development of organised and eventually public-funded elementary education in Blackburn in the second half of the nineteenth century. Those specifically catering for middle-class young ladies withered away a little later when girls' secondary education expanded.

Education for the masses got underway when the various religious bodies began to interest themselves more in education. Their first major involvement came with the Sunday school movement. The first Sunday school in Blackburn was opened by the Church of England in 1786 and catered for 300 children. Though limited to teaching religious knowledge, any study of the bible necessitated the children learning to read. Such schooling, therefore, was a great step forward for working-class children. Sunday school provision quickly began to grow though the three R's were not the spur.

Religious rivalry, to be analysed at length in Chapter 8, brought about the rapid growth of the Sunday school movement. By the end of the Napoleonic wars the Independents, the Baptists, the Methodists and the Roman Catholics had all decided to open Sunday schools. By 1824 the Church of England, though first in the race, had fallen behind in the provision of places. 1,100 children now attended Anglican Sunday schools weekly but 1,276 attended Nonconformist ones whilst a few others went to a Catholic school.

The coming of the Reverend Whittaker to Blackburn sparked off the Church of England counter-offensive. The expressed view of the Anglican Sunday school movement was to provide 'moral restraint' in a town where population growth had apparently outstripped civic authority.[5] The main motive was Whittaker's shock that the Church of England was being left behind in this field by the other churches. He now co-ordinated a town-wide offensive against such encroachment on what Whittaker saw as the home ground of the established church. The other religious bodies reacted by expanding as well. The result was that by 1875 Blackburn had a Sunday school population of 21,000 out of a total town population of 80,000. And what would have gladdened the heart of the Reverend Whittaker is that 9,500 of these went to Church of England Sunday schools. To his dismay he also would have noted that 8,000 attended a plethora of Nonconformist Sunday schools whilst 3,500 trooped off to Roman Catholic ones.

Not content with just having children on Sundays, the churches in Blackburn involved themselves in the voluntary day school movement. Again religious rivalry was the main motive behind expansion of provision. The Nonconformists were first off the mark. The Independents set up a Lancastrian school in Ainsworth street in 1810. The Church of England could not allow this to pass unnoticed. Within a year the Sunday school in Thunder Alley became a National day school.[6] By 1824 it taught up to 800 using the Madras system of pupil monitors. This was still the educational state of play for the Church of England when the energetic Reverend Whittaker came on the scene. Not just content with revitalising the Anglican Sunday school movement, working with the National Society he set about encouraging the expansion of the day school provision. The Nonconformists and the Roman Catholics, of course, had to follow suit. The result was that by 1870, when the Government passed Forster's Education Act in an attempt to give all children at least the chance of attending an elementary school, Blackburn boasted nineteen voluntary schools. And Whittaker could rest easy in his grave. Of the 13,073 children who attended these schools in 1871, 6,901 went to a Church of England school, 2,317 went to a Roman Catholic school whilst only 2,743 attended a Nonconformist voluntary school.[7] The established church was winning the educational race. Soon they would streak ahead.

The second element encouraging the growth of elementary education in Blackburn prior to 1870 was the town's employers. They first involved themselves in the Sunday school movement. Joseph Feilden donated land for such a school in the Billinge and Mile End area of the town. Joseph Eccles started a Sunday school at Stakes Hall in 1843.[8] In fact millowners financed virtually the whole of the Sunday school movement. The motive behind this benevolence was explained by the millowner John Baynes in 1857:

> Does not the experience of every manufacturer testify to the truth ..? Those workmen and workwomen who are the most sober, steady, respectable and intelligent have been, or still are, connected with the Sunday schools.[9]

The same motive, along with loyalty to the church to which they belonged and the fact that schooling would help to instill the value of discipline in pupils, was behind employer involvement in helping to finance the building of day schools. Self-interest also dictated that any such school would be in the vicinity of the benefactor's mill. This would allow a steady supply of basically educated labour and would also help ensure the gratitude and loyalty of their parents who would mainly be their employees. Eccles built a British Society school near his Nova Scotia mills in 1835. Hornby built one alongside his Brookhouse mills in 1839 and had his crest proudly and conspicuously carved in stone above the main entrance.

Again religious rivalry was obviously to the forefront of this spate of schoolbuilding. Hopwood built an Anglican school near his mills at Grimshaw Park in 1850 that later became Christ Church school. In the same year the Pilkingtons financed the building of a Congregationalist school virtually next door in Park Road.[10] Grimshaw Park, formerly deprived of voluntary schools, now had two appear in the space of a few months.

Religious rivalry within education was taken even further by many millowners. The Nonconformist James Briggs in 1880 took all the half-timers who worked at his mill out of the local Anglican school and sent them to one that he had just built. Robert Hopwood Hutchinson was publicly attacked in 1874 for only employing children from Church of England schools at his mills. In 1879 a rule at Boothman's 'Punch-noggin' mill stated quite openly that all children who worked there would attend the Anglican All Saints school and no other.[11]

But notwithstanding all these schools, Blackburn before 1870 still had a low literacy rate. A survey of marriage registers to find out how many in the town were capable of signing their names shows that in the period 1754–1777 33% could. Between 1800–1820 the figure had fallen to 31% whilst between 1850–1870 it was still only 45%.[12]

> Blackburn with its teeming population is at the present time behind every other town in England in intelligence, for it appears that out of every one hundred men only 39 can write their name; and out of 100 women only eleven are able to do so – while in London 89 men and 76 women out of every 100 are able to read and write.[13]

It must be realised that even the few who could sign their name may not have been able to write much else, a signature being the first and perhaps only writing skill that they would learn.

The partnership between major employers and the Anglican church reached its peak in the working of Blackburn's School Board established under the Education Act of 1870. Such Boards were ordered to ensure that

A classroom at Crosshill School circa 1920. Though taken just after the First World War this photograph gives an insight into the cramped classrooms that comprised the numerous Victorian schools that were a legacy dominating elementary and later primary education in Blackburn up to and beyond the Second World War. *Courtesy of Blackburn Library*

every child in their area of responsibility had a local elementary school to attend. If one was not available then they had to use ratepayers' money to provide one. There were 29 original candidates for the thirteen seats but pre-election agreements meant that no voting was needed. Cotton manufacturers were in the majority holding seven seats, with a Hornby in the chair. Churchmen held three seats. This ratio remained until the School Board was replaced by a Local Education Authority set up under the 1902 Education Act. The remaining School Board places were filled from the professions or even tradesmen towards the end of the century. The overall result, however, was a constant cotton/Anglican church majority, and it was a dominance that they used to good effect.[14]

In its 32 years of existence the School Board only used ratepayers' money to build three schools. A further existing school was taken over from a Nonconformist church. Most of the schools that Blackburn needed in order to allow all children in the town to attend elementary school had already been built by the churches, especially the Church of England. Co-operation was so close between the School Board and the churches that when it was decided that a school was needed in the Dukes Brow area, the School Board informed the Church of England of the fact and then delayed action until the Church authorities raised the necessary finance to build one. By 1900 church schools totally dominated elementary education in the town. 12,500 pupils attended the twenty-five Anglican schools, 6,350 the eleven Nonconformist schools and 4,350 the eight Roman Catholic schools; a total of 23,200 against only 1,500 pupils who attended the four Board schools.[15] Such figures are in stark contrast to those elsewhere in the north west. At Bolton average attendance at church schools was 14,540 compared to 10,056 at Board schools, whilst in Oldham only 8,236 attended church schools against the 11,099 who went daily to Board schools.[16] In Blackburn the middle-class cotton interest and the churches, especially the Church of England, had elementary education comfortably in their grip.

But for all this schoolbuilding, elementary education in Blackburn was not successful in educational terms, and it is the middle-class elite that must bear the brunt of the blame. Because the motives behind schoolbuilding were not mainly educational the consequence was that not enough attention was ever paid to educational results. It was not the quality of the teaching that was at fault but an ambivalent attitude towards education in general that grew up in the town.

One main reason for this was the strong tradition of half-time schooling in Blackburn under which children were released from factory work to attend school only part of each day. As noted in Chapter 2, child labour had always been an integral part of the cotton industry as far back as the domestic system of manufacture. It did not depart from the mills with the passing of the numerous Factory Acts. What these acts did was merely alleviate the conditions under which the children worked and limited the age range and working hours available to employers. Initially full-time education could cease at the age of eight after which child workers attended school only half-time. This minimum level was raised to ten soon after the Factory Act of 1874 and Sandon's Education Act of 1876. It rose to eleven in 1893 and twelve in 1899. In order to claim exemption from fulltime schooling after education was made compulsory in the town under the permissive clauses in the Education Act of 1870, parents officially had to apply to the local school board and show that their child had reached a certain standard of education. They were greatly encouraged by the Blackburn board, dominated by cotton manufacturers who fully supported the half-time system, who refused even to set a standard until forced to do

The Board School, Ewood, around 1890. Blackburn School Board, established under the Education Act of 1870, only used ratepayers' money to build three schools during its entire 32-year existence. Religious bodies, with the Church of England to the forefront, had a stranglehold on elementary education in the town, and the School Board approved of this and actively encouraged its continuance. When it was deemed that a school was needed in a certain part of the borough, then the Church of England was given the first chance of providing it. Only if they failed to do so did the Board have one built. *Courtesy of Blackburn Library*

so by the Board of Education in London in 1880. Even then they set it at the bare minimum. Education could not stand in the way of the hiring of labour. It was not until 1884 that the local school board reluctantly brought in a rule that an official certificate should be issued to early school-leavers to show that exemption had been formally granted, thus making the illegal employment of children far more difficult.[17]

The result was that in 1872 after education for 5–13 year olds had been made compulsory, 2,784 boys and 2,844 girls were half-timers. In 1902 2,110 boys and girls still were and in 1914 1,600. Blackburn had far more such children than other textile towns. In 1882 in the major industrial towns of Yorkshire and Lancashire an average of 10% of children were half-timers. In Blackburn it was 25%. It did not fall to 10% until 1902.

A shortage of school places for those that wanted them was never a problem in Blackburn, even though the Newcastle commission of 1858,

Pupils and teacher at Witton Park School, 1892. Elementary schools such as this were the sole providers of education for the overwhelming majority of Blackburn's children. Here they received instruction in the basic three R's. The children were then deemed sufficiently educated by both their parents and the town's elite for life and the mill.

Courtesy of Blackburn Library

Exemption Certificate given to thirteen year old girl in 1916. Being exempted from full-time education in order to work in the mills from an early age was traditional in Blackburn. In a town that had no tradition of education or culture, both the local elite and many of the parents encouraged the granting of such exemptions.

Courtesy of Blackburn Library

investigating the extent of working-class education, highlighted it as a national one when it reported. In 1871 there were 16,908 places available in the voluntary school sector but only 11,961 were filled. Their geographical spread was also adequate with only one school in the town found to have genuine overcrowding.[18] Even after elementary education was made compulsory for the town's children the place provision was more than adequate. In 1875 total accommodation had risen to 18,933 places but only 13,073 pupils were recorded as receiving at least some schooling. By 1901, as the Church of England carried on expanding its school provision in order to dominate elementary education in the borough, there was an excess of 7,000 places.[19]

The problem was that many children just did not go to school and of those that did attendance rates by both half-timers and full-timers left a lot to be desired. Just prior to the school board being set up in 1871, of the 17,453 children of school age in the borough only 12,807 were on the school registers. Many of these did not attend regularly. Of the 10,532 on the registers of publicly inspected schools an average of only 7,023 actually turned up daily. Three years after education was made compulsory attendance was no better. Of the 14,846 pupils attending inspected schools still only 9,609 came daily: a 35% absence rate.

Several reasons other than the support of the half-time system by the employer class help explain this poor attendance record and the general low esteem in which education was held by many of the populace of Blackburn. There was no tradition of education or culture in the town and, as will be seen, no self-improvement movement of any note. Parental pressure too was on the side of the half-time system. They even organised a School Grievance Committee to complain against the fact that parental income was being used as one yardstick in any decision about granting children exemption from full-time education. The parents also complained that doctors were stopping too many children on medical grounds from being given half-time status. Many of Blackburn's parents wanted their children in the mills as early as possible so that they could begin earning. The work ethic in this town was a factory one, not school based.

Poverty did not help. Not only was a child's wage needed but many parents could not afford to pay school fees which were among the highest in the north west. Though the 1870 Education Act allowed school boards to use rate money in place of school fees Blackburn's chose not to. In the late 1890s fees were still being paid in Board schools in the town when 93% of such schools in England and Wales had ended them. Until 1898 Blackburn also had a system whereby the Poor Law Guardians paid the fees of parents who could not afford them, not the school board. Though the board recommended which parents should receive financial help the Guardians insisted on a separate vetting and many parents avoided what they felt was the stigma of such an interview. The Poor Law Guardians were also far from generous. Of the 504 applicants for fee aid in 1872 only 287 were accepted.

The attitude of Blackburn's elite to education for the working classes is also shown in the number of attendance officers who were employed to enforce compulsory education. In 1882 a survey of the 22 largest northern towns revealed an average of one officer for 2,739 children. In Blackburn it was one per 4,199. It is little wonder that many children illegally avoided schooling.

Secondary education in Blackburn prior to 1914 was very limited. As noted earlier, a boys grammar school had been originally established in 1514 and received its present name when given a royal charter in 1567. The Taunton commission of 1869, investigating the national state of secondary education, reported that the school had 83 day pupils and thirteen boarders, that its buildings were in a poor condition and that it had a very poor record of university entrance.

It was, of course, a middle-class institution, only admitting three scholars a year from the town's elementary schools as late as 1894. By 1905 it still had only 137 on the school roll. One reason for the school's continued weakness was the lack of a large middle class in Blackburn to supply it with pupils. Another reason was that many of the town's middle class preferred a more modern curriculum for their sons rather than the classics served up at the grammar school; a curriculum geared to the skills they believed were more relevant to the modern world of commerce. For that reason, as noted in Chapter 3, many manufacturers chose to send their sons to private commercial academies. The main one was Hooles Academy which combined 'gentlemanly polish' with the 'distinctly commercial'.[20] Others preferred to send their sons away to boarding schools. The top families even chose public schools such as Harrow and Rugby. In 1871 217 of Blackburn's children were being educated outside the borough.

It was as a result of middle-class pressure that a Girls' High School was opened in 1883. Situated in a private house on Preston New Road it was modelled on those set up around the country by the Girls' Public Day School Company. With an entry age of nine, this school had 150 pupils within ten years and 210 by 1914. Its academic standing was not high. But then again this was not the main reason why Blackburn's middle class sent their daughters there.

> The School is scarcely of first grade character but owes its existence and such success as it attains to social considerations rather than to any superiority in the range and character of the educational advantages which it offers.[21]

For the parents it was the social standing that attendance conferred on their daughters that was of greatest importance, not academic standing.

Roman Catholic girls received a secondary education at the Convent of Notre Dame school founded in 1908. It was formed by joining together the Convent Higher Grade school and its pupil teacher centre. By 1914 it had 160 pupils aged 9–18. Academic success received a higher priority here since the school's main ambition was to turn out as many future Catholic schoolmistresses that it could to help make up a national shortage.

Only a few working-class children benefited from secondary education. It did not help that were all still largely fee-paying institutions in 1914. The Girls' High School allocated 10% of its annual intake to free scholarship places from 1903 in return for a grant from the new local education authority. In addition a total of 22 scholarship boys attended

Queen Elizabeth's Grammar School by 1905. Some were financed by charitable trusts, others by the L.E.A. Extended education for a few other working-class children was available and came in the form of four Higher Grade Schools all attached to established voluntary elementary schools. Nevertheless, the little secondary education that was available in Blackburn by 1914 was almost entirely a middle-class preserve.

Adult education never had a strong tradition in the town. Mechanics Institutes started to be developed nationally in the 1820s and 1830s. Attended mainly by skilled working men, these organisations put on educational classes, had a lending library and staged public lectures. Manchester's Mechanics Institute opened in 1824, Bolton and Warrington both got one in 1825, and Preston in 1828. Blackburn was one of the last towns in which one was established. That was as late as 1843. It was never as well attended as those in neighbouring towns. In 1850 Burnley's institute had 280 members and a lending library of over 3,000 volumes. In the same year Bolton had 282 members and 3,657 volumes. Blackburn had a mere 170 members and only 800 books.[22] There also were attempts to make church institutes into social and educational centres for young working-class men but this effort failed due to lack of interest.[23]

Government grants for evening class provision started in 1851 and expansion was encouraged by a number of following parliamentary acts. But Blackburn had no organised evening class provision until 1893. Before that date such classes were sporadic and transient. The school board had drawn up regulations for evening classes in 1872 but had never implemented them. In 1893 classes at last started at two board schools and at three voluntary schools. They offered the basic three R's and instruction in skills such as cookery and dressmaking. By 1900 there were fifteen centres and just under one thousand enrolments. By 1914, however, evening classes had developed into the main form of secondary schooling available to the majority of Blackburn's population. 3,500 students per annum were enrolling by 1914. The Workers Educational Association, formed nationally in 1904, backed by the trade union and co-operative movements, also opened up a branch in the town in 1909, assisted by Manchester University's Extra-Mural Department.

The only real success story was that of Blackburn Technical College. The foundation stone was laid in 1888, one year before an Act of Parliament was passed allowing rate money to be used for financing the building of such colleges. It was, therefore, one of the first to be opened in the country. The attitude of the town's employer class to this college compared to the one that they held for other forms of working-class education can perhaps be explained by the type of education that it

The Old Grammar School in Frecklington Street. Founded in 1514 and renamed Queen Elizabeth's Grammar School in 1567 when given a royal charter. Though it changed sites on more than one occasion it clung tenaciously to its role in educating a small number of boys from the families of the town's elite, even though the main families preferred to send their sons outside the borough to receive an education.

Courtesy of Blackburn Library

provided. It had building, chemical, engineering and textile departments. This was education for the masses that Blackburn's elite could appreciate. Well-funded, the college rewarded the support it was given. By 1914 it was deemed a centre of excellence by the Board of Education.

Overall the story of education in Blackburn before 1914 is disappointing. Thanks to millowner generosity, church competition and especially the determination of the Church of England to dominate elementary education in the borough, school places in the second half of the nineteenth century, unlike in many other towns, were always adequate to cope with demand. But the sad fact is that the demand for places did not match this availability. For that the town's elite must take the blame. It was they who failed to encourage a love of culture and a sense of the importance of education in the working classes. By vigorously supporting the half-time system, by adopting a lackadaisical attitude to school attendance and educational standards, and by not earlier encouraging evening class provision and self-improvement movements, they ensured that the working classes of Blackburn would put the importance of earning an early wage before an education: an ingrained attitude that would be taken into the twentieth century.

REFERENCES

1. Quoted in G.C. Miller, *Blackburn: Evolution of a Cotton Town*, Blackburn Town Council, Blackburn, 1951.
2. Report of Chester Diocesan Board of Education, 1839, (Blackburn Deanery) cited in B.J. Biggs, 'Education in Blackburn 1870–1914', unpublished MEd. dissertation, University of Durham, 1961.
3. Biggs, 'Education in Blackburn'.
4. A newspaper cutting of 1805 cited in Miller, *Evolution of a Cotton Town*.
5. Report of the Committee of Blackburn's National Society Schools, 1828, quoted in B. Lewis, *Life in a Cotton Town: Blackburn 1818–48*, Carnegie Press, Preston, 1985, p.60.
6. The National Schools were formed by the National Society for the Promoting of the Education of the Poor in the Principles of the Established Church set up in 1811. This was in answer to the schools, opened by the Royal Lancastrian Society formed in 1808 and renamed the British Foreign Schools Society in 1814, which took in all children regardless of religion and taught a christian education not tied to any particular church. They were, however, predominantly allied to the Nonconformists.
7. Extracted from Census of children made for Blackburn Board of Education, 1871, Blackburn Library Local History Collection.
8. Mill Hill Congregational Church Souvenir Handbook, 1921, in Blackburn Library Local History Collection.
9. D. Walsh, 'Working class development, control and new conservatism: Blackburn 1820–1850', unpublished MSc. dissertation, University of Salford, 1986.
10. C. Birtwistle, 'A history of the education of children in the Blackburn Hundred to 1870', unpublished MA dissertation, University of London, 1952, pp.121 and 141; collection of Church and Chapel Centenary booklets in Blackburn Library Local History Collection.
11. Biggs 'Education in Blackburn', and P. Joyce, *Work, Society and Politics*, Harvester Press, London, 1980.
12. Birtwistle, 'History of Education'.
13. Minute Book of Blackburn Mechanics Institute 1844–46, Blackburn Library Local History Collection.
14. Biggs, 'Education in Blackburn'.

15. G. Trodd, 'Political change and the working class in Blackburn and Burnley 1880–1914', unpublished PhD thesis, University of Lancaster, 1978.

16. Biggs, 'Education in Blackburn'.

17. Biggs, 'Education in Blackburn'.

18. Census of children.

19. Biggs, 'Education in Blackburn'.

20. A. Howe, *The Cotton Masters 1830–1860*, Clarendon Press, Oxford, 1984.

21. Board of Education Inspector quoted in Penny Summerfield, 'Cultural Reproduction in the Education of Girls: a Study of Girls' Secondary Schooling in Two Lancashire Towns, 1900–1950,' in Felicity Hunt (ed), *Lessons For Life: The Schooling of Girls and Women 1850–1950*, Basil Blackwell, Oxford, 1987, p.153.

22. J.W. Hudson, *History of Adult Education*, London, 1851, quoted in M.B. Smith, 'The growth and development of popular entertainment and pastimes in Lancashire cotton towns 1830–1870,' unpublished MLitt. thesis, University of Lancaster, 1970.

23. *Blackburn Standard*, 13 November 1867 and 16 December 1868.

7

Leisure
1750–1914

The reasons behind changing leisure activities during the industrial revolution have recently been a lively arena for debate amongst historians.[1] How far did pre-industrial leisure patterns, steeped in rural folklore, survive the move to an urban, industrial environment? If they disappeared, after how long, and was this as a result of deliberate suppression by the rapidly expanding and ever more powerful middle class? Did employers launch a direct attack on working-class leisure patterns in a bid to ensure that they did not intrude on a disciplined working week dictated by the factory bell? Were new leisure pursuits sponsored that were deemed more suitable companions for the new work ethic? It has also been suggested that many amongst the new middle classes encouraged 'rational recreation' for the working classes: new pursuits that would restore a common sense of community. It is claimed that these were encouraged by bodies such as town councils and churches.[2] Or were the main pressures, which brought about changing leisure pursuits in the new industrial towns and cities of the nineteenth century, simply the new urban conditions that were being experienced and the rise of a class-based society? On the other hand, it has been asked, did traditional leisure activities actively continue, perhaps in an adapted form? Did an independent working-class culture resist all blandishments and pressures and not only survive but prosper? It is against the background of this ongoing debate that the experience of the townspeople of Blackburn will be viewed.

Pre-industrial leisure in Lancashire revolved around religious festivals: Christmas, Shrove Tuesday, Mid Lent Sunday, Easter, Whitsun and local saints' days.[3] Drinking, dancing and the open door of hospitality for visiting friends and relations took central stage at these times. Social characteristics rarely alter overnight, so these holidays and the rural and traditional pursuits associated with them moved with the migrants into growing towns such as Blackburn. We will see that some were shortlived, that others survived for quite some years, but that most underwent some form of evolutionary experience.

Many rural pursuits were violent in nature, practised by the public and accepted and even supported by the elite. Bear baiting still took place in Blackburn market place in the 1760s. Bull baiting, dog fighting, badger baiting, cockfighting and ratting were all also seen in the town at this time and until much later. But by the 1840s most of these had died out. The cockpits, tolerated by the old elite, were officially closed in the 1830s, suppressed by order of Blackburn's new civic leaders, even though it was not outlawed nationally until 1849. Cockfighting, however, was resilient, evolving into a working-class pastime that refused to be stifled and consequently went underground. It apparently still survived until the early years of the twentieth century.[4] Coursing was legally tolerated, and in the last quarter of the nineteenth century all classes took part in it. At this time James Briggs, a Blackburn quaker millowner, won the sports main prize, the Waterloo Cup, as did the local brewer James Ward.

Steeplechasing was a rural sport that was re-adopted by the urban community after a break in time. Almost certainly it was resurrected with the encouragement of the new millocracy who, as has been seen in Chapter 3, modelled themselves on an imagined squirearchy. The first Blackburn steeplechase was held in 1839, starting at the Yew Tree Inn on Preston New Road. It was then held annually until 1844 behind the Bull's Head on Whalley Road, Wilpshire, attracting thousands of spectators and bridging the social divide.

Perhaps the most important influence on pre-industrial leisure patterns that was imported into the urban environment from the rural was that of religious festivals and the traditions that had grown up around them. In the north west this meant the 'wakes'. A 'wake' was a pre-industrial village or church feast celebrating the saint after whom the local church was named or the anniversary of the church's dedication. It originally took the form of an all-night vigil or 'waking'. It was most likely a christianised version of an earlier pagan observance. However, unlike neighbouring Whalley and Salmesbury, Blackburn did not have an ancient 'wake' tied to the saint's day of the parish church, or at least it was no longer celebrated. This was probably due to the local decline of the influence of the established church in the eighteenth century. The important consequence was that in Blackburn the timing of future holidays would be partly decided by the millowners and not by tradition and that though the term 'wake' would be used to describe the main annual holiday break it had nothing to do with any traditional saint's day.

Some religious customs, however, did survive, at least into the first half of the nineteenth century. Mummers' plays at most holy festivals and Pace or Pasch-egging prior to Easter Sunday were two of these. The latter was

'Bed of Stone', Waterloo Cup winner in 1872. For many of the town's elite who modelled their social habits on those of an imagined squirearchy, country pursuits were the ones to follow. A number of them enjoyed coursing and even proudly paraded winning dogs they owned on political platforms. As a result, whilst millowners in other towns perhaps left a Pre-Raphaelite painting behind them, James Briggs left a stuffed champion greyhound for the inhabitants of Blackburn to cherish.

Photo by Ian Beesley courtesy of Blackburn Museum

based around the egg, considered by Christians as representing both the universe and the resurrection. Children stained them red to symbolise the blood of Christ and various other bright colours to represent joy. Groups of masked young men, often dressed in mummers' costumes, went from door to door playing drums and fiddles, acting out small plays, and receiving eggs as presents. These were then taken to the fields on Easter Sunday and rolled until broken.

There are a number of reasons why such rural pursuits and traditions were transposed into the early nineteenth-century urban setting. Most migrants into Blackburn came only a short distance and therefore such people were less likely to undergo a severance of all links between town and country. In addition, even by the 1830s, handloom weavers working in their own cottages still outnumbered factory workers.

These rural pastimes and traditions, however, often soon changed or adapted to the new environment in which they found themselves. Pace-egging was one such example. By the 1840s, instead of asking householders for eggs the young men toured the public houses and demanded drink. Coursing was another. As has already been noted, middle-class employers kept up this pursuit, but the working classes could only afford to spectate. Their alternative, adapted to the urban environment, was whippet racing. These small dogs, with smaller appetites than greyhounds, could be reared, kept and raced in the backyards, alleys and streets of Blackburn.

Pigeon racing too was strong in Blackburn especially just prior to the First World War. This was another example of adapting a rural pursuit to urban conditions. This clinging to a rural past through leisure activities was noted by contemporaries:

> When the work of the day is done, whilst a percentage may go to a political club or in search of a reading room, that sort of thing is not the characteristic tendency of the average Blackburn man .... The one thing that distinguishes the Blackburn weaver from his fellows elsewhere in the country is his passionate love of sport. Nowhere do we find men so proud of a noted dog, so deeply concerned about a coursing match.[5]

But what was also happening was that the urban working class of Blackburn was developing its own, distinctive, leisure culture patterns.

Ballad singers and street performers were another rural hangover, but they also began to wither away. Ballad singers were the first to go when factory work increased in the 1830s and 1840s and as communication with the outside world improved and local newspapers flourished. By 1855 six had been started. Some were shortlived, but the *Blackburn Standard* lasted

Itinerant entertainers were common in the early part of the nineteenth century but by the time this photograph was taken at the turn of the twentieth century they were relatively rare. As working-class men and women came to have more disposable income to spend on leisure then the leisure industry grew to cater for their needs. As a consequence the street entertainers were no longer the attraction that they used to be.

Courtesy of Blackburn Museum

until 1904, and the *Blackburn Times* and the *Northern Daily Telegraph*, later the *Lancashire Evening Telegraph*, were still being read by an ever-increasing readership in 1914. Street performers lasted longer, even into the twentieth century, but the nineteenth century saw their protracted demise as indoor, commercial entertainment grew. There was a short revival in the cotton famine years of the 1860s but as employment returned the decline continued.

Memories of the soil even resurfaced over the years. A Floral and Horticultural Society was formed in 1850 that appears to have emanated without middle-class patronage, and was still flourishing in 1914. The rise of the allotment movement at the end of the century and during the Edwardian era was yet another sign of working-class greenfingers though this needed help in the form of the council setting aside land for the purpose. Whether this help falls into Peter Bailey's thesis of middle-class desire to promote from above the 'rational recreation' of the masses below is debatable. As we have seen in Chapter 3, by the turn of the twentieth century the make-up of the town council included a growing number of the shopocracy and even some of the skilled working class, and popular gardening may as legitimately be interpreted as an expression of working-class culture.

A clearer example of the encouragement of 'rational recreation' is the growth of municipal leisure facilities after the town was incorporated in 1851. Corporation Park covering fifty acres between Preston New Road to the crest of Revidge Hill was bought off Joseph Feilden in 1855 and opened in 1857. The total cost to the Corporation, since it also promised to build new roads to the east and west of the park, was £14,702. The old reservoirs had been turned into ornamental lakes, terraces and carriageways built, fountains installed and a battery built at the top of the hill to exhibit Crimean war cannon. Thousands attended the opening. The thirty-acre Queen's Park laid out in 1885 with three and a half acres of boating lake added to the town's amenities. Swimming baths were also provided. Freckleton Street baths were built in 1868 followed by baths at Belper Street in 1906 and Blakey Moor in 1911. But if this was the encouragement of 'rational recreation' to bring about a greater sense of shared community then it would have to have been carried out with the working classes in mind. In Blackburn's case this is not entirely certain. To take the example of Corporation Park, the fact that it was centred within the main middle-class residential district of the town and that it was designed with carriageways tends to point to the fact that it was intended to be mainly a middle-class playground.

Markets and fairs were also traditional events that had an influence on urban leisure. Market days, though mainly for the purchasing of goods, were also an occasion for drinking. These were kept though the traditional day of Monday on which they were held was altered by the town's elite. This was presumably to stem absenteeism and help break the pre-industrial habit of many of the working class of extending the weekend by taking 'Saint Monday' as a holiday.

The annual fairs were of greater influence in maintaining a continuation of leisure pursuits from the pre-industrial era, especially in a town like Blackburn that had no traditional 'wake' days. Such fairs were held three times a year: Easter Monday, two days at Whitsun and one day in October. Originally trading was the main function of these fairs with entertainment being of secondary importance. As an efficient transport system developed and with it improved shopping facilities, the trading aspect of fairs became of less importance to Blackburn's inhabitants. As a result pleasure fairs grew out of the old trading fairs. The main attractions of the Easter fair of 1849 showed the change. A large-headed girl, rabbit-eyed children and a lady giant topped the bill in the freak shows. Boxing, ring tossing, popgun shooting, wheels of fortune and sword swallowing made up a few of the sideshows. Those who showed animals joined together to form circuses and these started to visit Blackburn separately in the second half of the nineteenth century. In 1887

> Sanger's extensive circus and Hippodrome took up quarters in the Market Square. At noon on Monday (they) passed through the principal thoroughfares with a valuable stud of horses and accompanied by a band.[6]

There were other important changes to leisure habits, but these were consequent upon the imposition upon workers of a new industrial discipline. Over the north west as a whole, many saints' days were lost in the first half of the nineteenth century, as was the 'free Monday' or 'Saint Monday' traditionally taken by many self-employed handloom weavers. To ensure efficiency factory machinery had to be worked to capacity and therefore set factory hours had to be enforced and holidays reduced. Soon only Christmas day and Good Friday were left as holidays other than the summer 'wakes'. Such changes occurred in Blackburn with slight differences. Since Blackburn had no traditional 'wake' the inhabitants observed the Easter fair as the main holiday event. This in turn made Easter Monday the main holiday rather than Good Friday. In addition Whitsun remained important with its traditional Whit walks of pre-industrial origin. These were given added strength in the mid-nineteenth century as both church and chapel attempted to reassert the influence of religion on people's lives. Whit walks became a symbol of sectarian strength and parish pride and were still an essential feature of Whitsuntide celebrations in 1914.

Fair days too were slowly lost after 1850 both as holidays and events in themselves. Pleasure fairs began to meet opposition from various quarters including the 'respectable' middle classes, tradespeople and employers. As fairs grew to become increasingly working-class events in the mid-nineteenth century, and publicans' booths a common sight, the middle classes increasingly saw such crowds that were attracted as a danger to public morality and to public order. Market traders complained that they were thrown off their pitches for the duration and shopkeepers claimed that they lost custom. Employers found themselves plagued by absenteeism at fair times and also disliked having intermittent holiday periods forced on them.

Various Acts of Parliament slowly gave such opposition groups the powers that they needed. The 1847 Markets and Fairs Act and the 1858 Local Government Act gave councils the ability to create and regulate new fairs. The Fairs Acts of 1868, 1871, 1873 and 1878 then gave them the right to limit or even abolish existing fairs. By the 1880s Blackburn council had used these Acts to rid the town of the October cattle fair and reduce the

Easter fair from eight to four days. In addition they had used the 1874 Licensing Act to make fairs 'dry'. Now the employers turned their sights on ending the Easter fair entirely. Their main motive was to obtain agreed regular holidays for the town. They wanted to abolish the Whitsuntide holiday and turn Easter into the main break. They hoped that such a switch would reduce absenteeism. The fair stood in the way, encouraging people to remain in Blackburn instead of making Easter the time for annual trips and therefore the main holiday period in the minds of the people. But the banning of the fair from its town centre site in 1890 merely led to it finding a new site on private land belonging to the Feilden family. It even got larger, attracted yet more people and was no longer limited to an 11 p.m. finish. By 1893 the council surrendered and allowed it to return to the centre of the town. The small businessmen and traders, fretting over the fact that the moving of the fair had cost them more trade than keeping the fair on its original spot, outvoted the millowners. Tradition had kept its foothold.[7]

This attempt by the employers to reorganise the holiday calendar highlights one other change that urbanisation later brought to leisure patterns; that of increased yet designated leisure time. At first such time was actually restricted. Factory hours meant that until the 1840s the only time that millworkers had free was Sundays and after 8.30 p.m. on weekdays. The 1850 Factory Act then limited the working hours of women to between 6 a.m. and 6 p.m. and work on Saturdays finished at 2 p.m. Men gained as a consequence of this, but most daylight hours were still taken up by work. The net result was that leisure activities that could be pursued in the evenings grew. As will be seen, the theatre and the public house adapted to this need. With the growth of the free Saturday afternoon in the second half of the century yet further changes to leisure occurred, the rise of playing or watching sport being one.

Blackburn's new middle-class elite initially also restricted the number of holidays that the town's workers enjoyed, but were forced to give way mainly by national legislation but also by negotiation with the growing trade union movement within the town. Mills in Blackburn only stopped for four days on average in the 1830s. The lack of a traditional 'wake' cost Blackburn workers dear compared to neighbouring towns. Small gains were made in the years that followed, but the main breakthrough came with the passing of the 1871 Bank Holiday Act. This added Easter Monday, Whit Monday, Boxing day and the first Monday in August to Christmas day and Good Friday. At first Blackburn partly ignored the Act with the mills refusing to close on August Bank holiday. Even bank clerks in Blackburn failed to obtain the day off at first. But this was only a Canute-like gesture by Blackburn's millocracy.

In 1889 the millowners agreed with the unions that the Whitsun holiday be abolished in favour of three days at Easter and a full week in July at the time of the Darwen Fair. Pressure from below in the form of absenteeism meant that the Whit Monday and Tuesday were regained in 1891 in return for a shortening of the Easter and Summer breaks. Soon Whit Tuesday was traded in to make a full week in summer which was transferred to the second week in August. Most millworkers now received nine or ten days holiday a year. Blackburn's holidays were now set; the consequence of a mixture of tradition, Government legislation and millowner and trade union pressure.

The initial very long working hours for six days a week had meant that leisure time was largely confined to the evenings. As a result the theatres and the public houses adapted themselves to the demands made on them. The first record of a theatre in Blackburn is the Blackburn New Theatre in 1787 in Market Street Lane, though its name suggests that it was not the first. This theatre was later known as the Old Lyceum Theatre. In 1816 the Theatre Royal and Opera House was built in Ainsworth Street. Built of stone with three entrances, it had both a gallery and a pit. A further theatre opened in 1818. However, in the first three decades of the nineteenth century these theatres catered mainly for the middle classes since the long working hours of the working classes precluded their attendance. In the 1820s they were 'fashionably attended'. By the 1830s, as the factory class expanded and hours of work were marginally reduced, the clientele became more and more working class with a consequent change in the entertainment offered. At first the evening was divided into three, a comedy play, songs and a farce. Comic intervals between these sections became so popular with the growing influx of working-class patrons, that they developed into complete performances. Commercial pressure to offer a programme that the working classes wanted ensured that the Lyceum Theatre was converted to a 'music hall' in 1851. Theatres built after that were dedicated to a working-class clientele from the start. The Palace Theatre was built as a music hall on the site of an old Wesley Mission in Jubilee Street in 1899, but though it failed within a year, it was soon bought up and opened a year later as part of the MacNaughton Vaudeville Circuit. Its gallery was the largest in Lancashire, seating 1,000 people at just 2d a ticket, a price that shows the clientele for whom it catered. The Theatre Royal was also converted to a music hall in the years just prior to the First World War.[8]

The public house too adapted to the needs of its patrons. The encouragement of beer drinking under the 1830 Beer Act, as an antidote to spirit drinking, coincided with the growth of the power loom in Blackburn and the consequent rapid increase of factory workers. By 1862 there were

The Theatre Royal and Opera House in Ainsworth Street. Built in 1816, it originally catered for a mainly middle-class clientèle as did others at that time. However, once the working classes began to enjoy more leisure time as working hours decreased then the second half of the century saw such theatres begin to cater for the more raucous followers of the new music hall. *Courtesy of Blackburn Library*

462 drink outlets in the borough: one for every 23 houses. The number of beer shops reached a peak in 1868 with 309, whilst the number of public houses continued to grow: 183 in 1865, 225 in 1870, 249 in 1879 and 255 in 1892.[9] By that last date there were also 208 beershops, 106 off-licenses and 35 wine, spirit and sweet licenses: one license for every 34 houses in the borough.[10]

Because of the weakness of Nonconformism in Blackburn which the following chapter will show, the local middle class, unlike that in some neighbouring towns, encouraged the drink trade. This can be seen when the 1872 Licensing Act was passed. This Act gave magistrates the power to close public houses at 11 p.m. Only two towns in England did not take advantage of this. Blackburn was one, keeping its midnight closing hour.

WILPSHIRE.

The Wilpshire Hotel circa 1900. The public house played an integral part in working-class leisure during the nineteenth century. The reason for choosing this particular photograph is partly because it shows how little some public houses have changed over the last century and partly because it happens to be my local. In this age of the horse-drawn vehicle this picture also shows how filthy the roads were. In many contemporary photographs the horse dung has often been politely erased.

Courtesy of Blackburn Library

Given the relative weakness of Nonconformism in the town it is not surprising to learn that the Temperance movement was never strong in Blackburn. Even the opening of the Lees Hall Mission in St. Peter's Street in 1891 failed to rouse the movement. By 1913 the average attendance at meetings there was only 78.

That drink had become an integral part of nineteenth-century working-class culture in Blackburn was widely recognised.

> Strong drink is the secret of its own and Britain's greatness. Be sober, and lead a decent and respectable life and your genuine Blackburner will wax red at the mention of your name, and dismiss you as a '—— Dissenter'.[11]

Hal Whitehead, a local folk hero, took his love of drink to extremes. He is reputed to have drunk six and a half gallons of ale at the Britannia tavern in Lord Street in just five hours.

The *Blackburn Times* in 1891 noted that the new political working-men's clubs were often little more than drinking dens with a billiard table and bowling green attached. It also noted that in the main area for public houses around King Street and Northgate, they were as common 'as blackberries on a hedge'.[12] In 1896 26 out of the 38 trade societies in Blackburn held their meetings in public houses.

Drink, and especially the public house, remained a central feature of working-class popular leisure, one that remained unchanged from pre-industrial times. Blackburn's mainly Anglican, Conservative-dominated, middle-class elite made little or no move to limit it. Perhaps the only change that occurred was that drinking became more than ever class-based. The middle classes kept to their own taverns and clubs or drank at home.

More and more public houses now catered solely for working-class custom. Noting the growing success of the theatre in attracting working-class audiences, a number of enterprising landlords began to stage various forms of variety shows in the early 1840s. Some of the larger public houses, especially in Shorrock Fold and Darwen Street, began to have a 'music hall' or 'singing saloon' attached to the premises. Such places had the advantage of offering alcohol with the entertainment, something that the theatres of the day were unable to do. Entertainers were hired from as far away as Manchester. This form of entertainment was popular on a Saturday night with young working-class men and women, especially those earning regular wages at the factories. Competition between public houses now intensified with each trying to offer something different. The Star and Garter in 1851 installed a new self-acting organ complete with mahogany frame and see-through front. This played continuous tunes. Even at the end of the century most public houses relied heavily on music licenses to attract custom.[13] All this represented part of a new independent working-class culture being formed in the urban environment.

Working-class leisure patterns, including musical ones, were, however, also influenced by middle-class intervention. From the 1840s millowners encouraged the formation of works brass bands. In 1841 Messrs Hornby and Kenworthy built a walled gymnasium on land close to Whalley Road at their Brookhouse mills. It provided for football, tennis ball, skittles and quoits among other pastimes. This encouragement by the millowners of leisure pursuits for their workers became especially widespread in the second half of the nineteenth century.

Treats and trips became more common. One of the first was a dinner given by Hornby to his operatives to commemorate the opening of the gymnasium. Such treats then proliferated. Annual mill 'do's' were expected and given. For major events major treats were given. These could be on the occasion of an owner's son coming of age, a family wedding or even funeral. In 1853 1,900 operatives sat down to a feast paid for by W. H. Hornby. Mills were encouraged to have their own social committees that organised trips, socials, football and cricket matches and sports days. Railway excursion treats started in Blackburn in 1852/3 with workers thereafter often being taken to the seaside for the day.[14]

The motives of millowners in setting up and often financing such trips, treats or leisure facilities is difficult to pin down. The historian Patrick Joyce claims they were part of a new industrial paternalism that grew up in the 1840s, based on the image of the old tory squire: a form of urban *noblesse oblige*.[15] This leisure provision by the employers had a number of aims. It was partly a deliberate attempt at social control to keep the working classes happy with their lot, and to divert them from potentially more dangerous thoughts and paths. It was also felt that a fit, deferential and grateful workforce would be an economic asset.

Middle-class attempts to mould working-class leisure habits did not end here. From the 1870s a new generation of the industrial and professional middle classes introduced and encouraged team games among Blackburn's male working class. Often educated at public school, unlike their fathers before them, these young men returned to Blackburn imbued with the public school ethos of 'play up, play up, and play the game'. They believed that team sports moulded the character, bred loyalty and team spirit and encouraged self-esteem which in turn could be utilised for self-advancement. It was also healthy and would help counter the growing worry that physical deterioration amongst the lower classes would lead to Britain declining as the major industrial power and even as an empire.

Most of Blackburn's middle-class young men had been educated at schools where soccer was the main winter sport. This partly explains why Blackburn had to wait until 1920 before rugby union was introduced and why the town has no rugby league tradition. Soccer was different. Blackburn already had a footballing tradition that went back to the seventeenth century. By the 1870s the football that was played was the Harrow game, a cross between soccer and rugby and also played by A. N. Hornby and other youths of the town. 1875 saw Association Football introduced and the birth of Blackburn Rovers F.C. The club was formed at the St. Leger Hotel by a doctor and a number of ex-public and ex-grammar schoolboys. By 1878 Blackburn had 28 clubs including Blackburn Rovers, Blackburn Christchurch, Livesey United, Blackburn Park Road, Blackburn St. George and Blackburn St. Mark's. Virtually all the administration was carried out by ex-public schoolboys, and the heavy influence of church and chapel can also be noted. Cricket too was encouraged. Blackburn already had a team in the 1840s, but in the last quarter of the nineteenth century teams sprang up everywhere, again with mainly middle-class administrators at the helm.

Seen partly as a means of cultivating local patriotic spirit, and a way of instilling a sense of civic pride in Blackburn's populace, in addition to providing a fitter and healthier working class, this movement certainly seems to have worked. When Blackburn Olympic won the F.A. Cup in 1883 the team was carried on its return in a wagonette pulled by six horses and escorted by brass bands. Cheered by thousands thronging the streets, the whole team was then entertained that evening by the town's two Members of Parliament. Sadly the club soon folded. It was one of the few with working-class origins. Based on a working-men's club, its failure was mainly because it did not have the financial and organisational support of middle-class members as did clubs like Blackburn Rovers.

For many of the same reasons that soccer and cricket were encouraged by the town's middle class, so were such pastimes as whippet racing, pigeon racing and crown green bowling. All were seen by the employing and professional classes as respectable sports. It was only when attempts were made to move whippet racing down south that it gained its future unsavoury image. But these sports were different from soccer and cricket, for they were self-generated from within the working class and were further expressions of a separate, independent working-class culture that evolved during urbanisation. The reason that Blackburn's middle class encouraged such sports as these, as well as the team games and the working-men's clubs, was that working-class members had an hierarchical administrative structure to climb. Climbing it gave men and their families social pre-eminence and respectability. Such pastimes may have been part of an independent working-class culture but it was a form of culture of which the town's middle class approved. In their eyes it all helped to civilise the crowd.

It may be thought that the encouragement of 'respectable' sports, and the public school inspired evangelical spirit exhibited by the new middle-class generation, might have lowered class barriers at least in the sporting arena. In fact, in spite of paternalism the opposite occurred. In the second half of the nineteenth century class divisions were intensified and done so purposely in some cases.

Music exclusively for the middle classes existed in Blackburn. Serious music for the town's new elite was provided at the Angel Inn on King Street in 1837, whilst a Gentlemen's Glee Club was founded at the King's Arms in Northgate in 1849. A Handel Society flourished from 1752 to 1865. The performance of 'Joshua' in 1851 to an audience paying 7/6d (37.5p) a ticket shows the clientele it catered for.[16]

Blackburn Rovers F. C. 1879–1880. Though Blackburn Olympic were the town's first successful soccer club, winning the F. A. Cup in 1883, it was Blackburn Rovers who survived and prospered since that club had middle-class financial backing unlike Blackburn Olympic which had working-class origins. *Courtesy of Blackburn Library*

The middle classes had always had their own exclusive clubs. The Union club, founded in 1849, occupied part of Henry Sudell's original town house in Church Street. This gentlemen's club was followed by two political clubs in 1864. There was the Reform club for gentlemen of Liberal politics in Victoria Street near the new market place, built with an Italianate frontage, and the Conservative club in King William Street. In addition there was the County club in New Market Street. For Conservative and Liberal supporters of a lower social class there were the new and separate working-men's clubs built in the last quarter of the century.

These latter clubs often had crown bowling greens attached. The main families of the town, however, kept to their own Blackburn Subscription Bowling Club. In the early eighteenth century it was to be found at the foot of Cicely Hole. It moved in 1844 when the new railway company wanted the land as part of their railway station. Until the 1860s it was near the old Free Grammar School next to St. Peter's Church, before it finally moved to its present site on Shear Bank Road. At some time or other most of Blackburn's gentry belonged to it: the Feildens, Sudells and Cardwells

Blackburn Subscription Bowling Club c.1880. This club, dating from the eighteenth century, kept its membership limited and exclusive to the town's elite throughout the nineteenth century. At one time or another virtually every leading family had someone who belonged to it. *Courtesy of Blackburn Library*

followed by the Hornbys, Thwaites, Osbaldestons, Liveseys, Pilkingtons, Walmsleys and the Birleys. The membership was a roll call of the most influential Blackburn families. Membership was also strictly limited: 100 maximum as late as 1875.

It was no different in the years up to 1914. Introducing team sport to the masses was one thing, actually playing with or against them was another. The preference was either to form your own team from within your own social circle and play your own kind as happened in cricket, or to retreat into exclusive sports such as golf, hockey or lawn tennis. Safely and deliberately surrounded by high subscriptions and membership quotas, middle-class sportsmen avoided working-class intrusion.

The first method was practised by the East Lancashire Cricket Club. Founded in 1863/4 on the Alexandra Meadows by a group of officers from the local Volunteer Force, it was the third cricket club in Blackburn. Solidly middle class and based around a nucleus of the Hornby family, it maintained its exclusive membership through ballot and blackballing. The club played matches all over Lancashire but carefully avoided playing the two other local clubs with their rather questionable social mix. In 1868 they were prepared, however, to play the touring Australian Aboriginal team.[17]

Examples of the second defence against sporting miscegenation can be seen in local golf and hockey. Blackburn Golf Club was founded in 1894 hard on the heels of new clubs at Pleasington and Wilpshire. Using rented land on Revidge Heights, limiting the membership to 70 and charging an annual subscription of two guineas, the lower orders were kept at bay. A Mr. A. Greenwood, prominent cotton manufacturer, first club captain and chief driving force behind the founding of the club, saw to that.[18]

Blackburn Hockey Club, originally founded as Brownhill Hockey Club in 1904 on a field behind the Hare and Hounds at Lammack, was started by Herbert Troop, a young brewer. The idea originated during a discussion with a group of young middle-class friends who also played a little soccer. They all 'felt the urge to get out of the commonplace into a more distinctive game'. The first two vice-captains give a flavour of the successfully nurtured social level of the club: Alfred Livesey of the firm of loom makers of that name and Miss C. Bailey the daughter of the Borough Treasurer.[19]

Soccer was abandoned as a participation sport by the middle classes as the working classes took over both as players and spectators. The game now became imbued with working-class values and was incorporated into a separate popular culture that became more and more socially distinct from middle-class recreational habits. 8,000 watched Blackburn's football and cricket clubs joint sports day in 1875 and 10,000 watched Blackburn Rovers play Darwen in 1880. Crowd violence did not help keep the middle classes in the game. The 1880 match against Darwen was abandoned when the crowd, incensed at foul play, invaded the pitch. Ten years later in 1890, during the same fixture, the crowd not only invaded the pitch but destroyed the goalposts and ransacked the grandstand. The ex-public schoolboys had apparently omitted to teach the working classes how to be good losers.

The professionalisation of soccer has often been cited as one reason for the middle-class exodus from the game. Yet was there a full split? On the playing field perhaps but not on the administrative side. What had started out as being a way of bringing healthy sport to the masses and inculcating team spirit had become big business with ever increasing gate receipts as rising standards of living allowed workers to spend a greater proportion of their income on leisure activities. In addition there was the prestige and high public profile to be gained from being connected to a successful football club. What middle-class entrepreneur would turn his back on that? Is it any wonder that the north of England, the cradle of capitalism, was also the cradle of professional soccer, the greatest of spectator sports? Blackburn, led by its middle-class elite, took its part in that.

In 1884, after the F.A. at first refused to sanction professionalism, it was a meeting of the Lancashire clubs in Blackburn that exerted successful pressure by founding the shortlived, rival British Football Association. Blackburn Rovers was also the first club to lure Scots footballers south of the border with the offer of a team place and a well-paid supplementary job. Blackburn was at the forefront of forcing the F.A. to accept professionalism, and at the forefront of Blackburn Rovers was Blackburn's industrial and professional middle classes. As one commentator wrote:

> The exalted position attained by the Rovers F.C. in sporting circles is due not only to the players who have distinguished themselves on the field but to the fine example set by the gentlemen who have guided its destinies.[20]

These 'gentlemen' in 1895 included the two sitting MPs W. Coddington and W. H. Hornby, John Rutherford JP, and E. S. Morley MD JP. These are just some examples of the cotton manufacturers and professional men at the helm of the club.[21]

That Blackburn's middle classes were not against professionalism *per se* is even shown by the exclusive East Lancashire Cricket Club. From the start they employed two professionals , one lured from Blackburn Cricket club and the other from Yorkshire.[22] Winning was also important to Blackburn's middle classes.

The commercialisation of sport and other leisure pursuits would not have been possible without a massive improvement in communications.

A. N. Hornby. This member of the millowning Hornby family was one of the greatest of the town's nineteenth-century all-round sportsmen. He was a founder member of East Lancs. Cricket Club which studiously avoided playing local working-class opposition and kept their social purity through ballots and blackballing. *Courtesy of Blackburn Museum*

Trams at home football and cricket matches and railways offering cheap excursion tickets for away matches allowed not only teams to travel but spectators. Saturday afternoon sport gained in popularity up to 1914. Attendances at Blackburn Rovers home matches by this date were comfortably averaging in five figures, and their supporters also swelled the crowds at away matches. Crown green bowling also attracted large crowds. Competitions such as the Talbot from 1873 and the Waterloo from 1907 brought ever increasing entries and support. The Talbot's 84 entries in 1882 swelled to 1,000 by 1910, many being from professionals.

Blackpool, approximately 30 miles away, also found itself receiving thousands of spectators from all over Lancashire including Blackburn. Holiday outings by rail in the 1850s on four day or weekly tickets were mainly the prerogative of the town's middle classes. The working classes of Blackburn had to be satisfied with day excursions though this allowed trips further afield than had been possible on the Leeds–Liverpool canal outings that they had previously enjoyed. However, by the 1870s, as living standards improved, the working classes began to take prolonged seaside holidays, and during the 1880s and 1890s the tradition for weekend and weekly holidays gathered strength. Mills and public houses nearly all set up 'Going-off Clubs' between 1880 and 1914. These allowed families to save for their annual holiday outings. A deserted Blackburn became the symbol of holiday weeks rather than a crowded one.

Any discussion of Blackburn's leisure pursuits would not be complete without mentioning the Blackburn poets. This was not an oral tradition, for nearly fifty separate poets born before 1880 had their poems published. The earliest of the authors was born at the close of the eighteenth century but most in the 1840s and 1850s. This meant that it was an urban phenomenon and one that had its heyday in the last quarter of the nineteenth century. Most emanated from the working classes and most were power loom workers. It was a 'popular' culture in the truest sense and has to be seen as yet another part of an independent, urban working-class culture. There was even a poets' corner near Blakey Moor where, presumably, public recitations took place.[23] The movement mostly died away by 1914 as working-class leisure pursuits moved outside the home and away from the public house. Its legacy is a reminder that leisure patterns can be localised as well as being part of regional or national trends.

Leisure in early twentieth century urban Blackburn was certainly different from that experienced in earlier rural times. But it was not entirely distinct and separate. Traditional festivals, fairs, markets, games and sports all helped mould the leisure patterns and habits of urban Blackburn. Admittedly completely fresh leisure pursuits, such as the music hall and professional soccer, also grew in this new environment. Encouragement and ideas also came from the new middle classes thrown up by the industrial revolution. Their motives were mixed and they changed over time. The need for a disciplined workforce merged with paternalism and the desire for grateful and loyal employees. These motives in turn intermingled with attempts to produce a healthier working-class imbued with team spirit and one with what some deemed 'civilised' leisure pursuits. Even so by 1914 leisure was more class based than it had been in pre-industrial society. A distinct urban working-class culture had emerged, partly moulded by the town's middle class, but mostly emanating from within the working class itself. The emergent middle classes too purposely isolated themselves from the popular culture of the town as part of the process of erecting new social barriers to protect their newly won position. But what also superficially appears in 1914 to be a culture totally different from 150 years before was in reality one that owed much of its present form to pre-industrial roots.

REFERENCES

1. R.W. Malcolmson, *Popular Recreations in English Society 1700–1850*, Cambridge University Press, Cambridge, 1977; Peter Bailey, *Leisure and Class in Victorian England: Rational Recreation and the Contest for Control*, Routledge & Kegan Paul, London, 1978; Hugh Cunningham, *Leisure in the Industrial Revolution 1780–1880*, Croom Helm, London, 1980; J.M. Golby & A.W. Purdue, *The Civilisation of the Crowd*, Batsford, London, 1984.
2. Bailey, *Leisure and Class in Victorian England*.
3. John Walton & Robert Poole, 'The Lancashire Wakes in the Nineteenth Century' in Robert Storch ed., *Popular Culture and Custom in Nineteenth Century England*, Croom Helm, London and Canberra, 1982.
4. *Blackburn Times*, 23 January 1904.
5. *Cotton Factory Times*, 1 June 1888.
6. *Blackburn Standard*, 10 May 1887.
7. R.J. Poole, 'Wakes, Holidays and Pleasure Fairs in the Lancashire Cotton District c.1790–1890', unpublished PhD thesis, University of Lancaster, 1985.
8. G.J. Mellor, *The Northern Music Hall*, Graham, Newcastle, 1970.
9. Chief Constable's Annual Reports in Blackburn Library Local History Collection.
10. W.E. Moss, *Life of Mrs. Lewis*, Epworth Press, London, 1926.
11. *Free Lance (Manchester)* 12 October 1867, quoted in Patrick Joyce, *Work, Society and Politics*, Harvester Press, London, 1980.
12. *Blackburn Times*, 22 August 1891.
13. *Blackburn Times*, 22 August 1891.
14. Joyce, *Work, Society and Politics*.

15. Joyce, *Work, Society and Politics*.
16. Janet M. Geddes, 'Music in Blackburn', Dissertation for unknown H.E. Institution, 1958, in Blackburn Library Local History Collection.
17. Souvenir Booklet of East Lancashire Cricket Club Bazaar, 1929, Blackburn Library Local History Collection.
18. History of Blackburn Golf Club, 1954, Blackburn Library Local History Collection.
19. Fifty Years of Hockey in Blackburn 1904–1954, Blackburn Library Local History Collection.
20. C. Francis, History of Blackburn Rovers F.C. 1875–1925, Toulmin, Blackburn, 1925.
21. Blackburn Rovers F.C. Bazaar Booklet, 1895, Blackburn Library Local History Collection.
22. East Lancs. Souvenir Booklet.
23. B. Morris, 'The Growth and Development of Popular Entertainment and Pastimes in Lancashire Cotton Towns 1830–1870', unpublished MLitt. thesis, University of Lancaster, 1970.

8

Religion
1750–1914

Since Saxon times St. Mary's church has stood at the heart of Blackburn. For centuries it catered for the religious needs of the surrounding community. When cotton caused the comparatively sudden growth of Blackburn the parish church found itself floundering as urbanisation brought in not only tens of thousands more people but also an influx of Catholic Irish and the competition of Nonconformism. The virtual monopoly of the Church of England was being threatened. The nineteenth century was to see a religious struggle for the souls of the population; a struggle partly seen in attempts to increase the size of their respective congregations; partly in the effect it had on the working and leisure hours of the community; and partly in the educational and political arenas.

The revival of the Church of England was late in starting. It was begun by the Reverend John William Whittaker who was appointed vicar of Blackburn in 1821. At this time the population of the town was 21,940 which meant the ancient church of St. Mary's, together with St. John's (1789) and the newly built St. Peter's, each ministered to an average of over 7,000 inhabitants. By 1831 St. Paul's had been added to the C of E fold but the ratio had hardly altered, since the population had risen to over 27,000.

The late 1830s saw Whittaker initiate plans for three new churches. His success was limited. Only Holy Trinity at Mount Pleasant was built by 1846, though an old Wesleyan chapel was bought at Daisyfield. This was later demolished to make way for St. Michael's and All Angels. The next vicar, Dr. John Rushton, in the second half of the 1850s began a second attempt at extending the realm of the established church. By now the population was rising to over 60,000. Christ Church at Grimshaw Park was built in 1859 and St. Thomas at Bottomgate in 1865. All Saints at Nova Scotia was finally completed in 1872. Further churches then appeared intermittently until there were fourteen Anglican churches in the borough by 1892.

One reason for the comparatively slow start by the Church of England to assert itself may be explained by the fact that Nonconformism was late in gaining a firm foothold in Blackburn. John Wesley made twenty visits to north-east Lancashire between 1747 and 1790, but though he often preached in Lower Darwen, speaking there as early as 1759, he always hurried through Blackburn. It was not until 1780 that he felt it safe enough to preach there for the first time. As his diary states: 'In the afternoon we went to Blackburn .... All the chief men of the town were there. It seemed as the last shall be first'.[1]

The first methodist chapel soon followed in Clayton street in 1786 in 'the most respectable part of the town ... surrounded by gardens and the houses of the leading tradesmen'.[2] It replaced the first preaching house in Old Chapel Street near Salford bridge off Penny Street that Wesley had opened on his first visit. But by 1809 the local society still had only 198 members, and this included the thriving community in Lower Darwen. When this is compared to the 98 in the nearby village of Mellor the limited early impact of Wesleyanism is seen in perspective.

Other dissenting groups also attempted to put down roots in Blackburn. In the early eighteenth century, many Scottish 'chapmen' settled here and an independent chapel was built in Chapel lane in 1778. A Baptist preacher visited as early as 1726, and a society was formed in Blackburn in 1760 with a chapel being constructed in 1766 at Islington croft on the edge of the town's moor, the first purpose built Nonconformist building in Blackburn. Quakers, Presbyterians and Primitive Methodists followed. Other small movements came and went. Kilhamites and Jerusalemites in the Eanam area, a Swedenborgian chapel in Ainsworth street, a Ranters' chapel, a Unitarian meeting house and even a small group of Mormons. In variety Nonconformism was large: in number, however, relatively small.

Roman Catholicism also was not strong in Blackburn in the early years of the nineteenth century. It is thought that the first public Catholic church was a plain brick building hidden away among houses between King Street and Chapel Street and built in 1773. It was closed when St. Alban's church was built at Larkhill in the mid 1820s. Three others followed in the mid-nineteenth century: St. Anne's in France Street (1849–51), St. Mary's (1864–65) and St. Joseph's at Higher Audley (1875). In addition the Sisters of Notre Dame purchased Brookhouse lodge in 1859 for a convent. It is estimated that by 1820 there were approximately 1,200 Catholics in Blackburn rising to 3,000 in 1851. The small but growing Irish community was its base.

Even by the mid-nineteenth century, though Catholicism and Nonconformism had grown, the Church of England was still dominant. Perhaps the best measure of the relative strengths of the religious groups at this juncture is to be seen by studying the burials in the municipal cemetery, most church and chapel churchyards having overflowed by the mid-nineteenth century.

Rev. Dr. John William Whittaker, Vicar of Blackburn 1822–1854. On the advent of Nonconformism and Catholicism to Blackburn, this was the man who took it upon himself to begin the battle for the souls of the inhabitants against the followers of Wesley and of Rome.

Courtesy of Blackburn Library

Interments in 1866 are typical of that decade: C. of E. 1,482, Nonconformists 322 and Roman Catholics 303.

The early dominance of the Anglican church may have been a major factor in its late start in churchbuilding, but competitive fear was certainly to the fore when it finally began. To be fair a missionary spirit was one reason, though it needed spurring on by the threat of competition for the souls of the masses. The Rev. Whittaker saw an urgent need for a church in the Daisyfield area because 'close to this place is the Popish Chapel'. As for the need for Holy Trinity Church this was necessitated by the possibility of a breakaway group of Independents building a chapel in the Mount Pleasant area which would give them a free run in the conversion stakes. 'To prevent this,' Whittaker wrote to the Archbishop of Canterbury, 'and with the further view of attracting malcontents to the church, I am extremely anxious to have the start of them.'[3]

Throughout his term of office, which ended in the mid 1850s, Whittaker kept 21 local churches under the patronage of St. Mary's. The reason for this centralisation of power was to ensure no schism could occur that might interrupt the fight against Nonconformism and Catholicism. Dr. Rushton, his successor, carried on the good fight. It was no coincidence that, after years of neglect, the foundation stone of Christ Church at Grimshaw Park was laid on Whit Monday only a few short weeks after the foundation stone was laid of a new chapel in Park Street on Good Friday.

The building of churches, however, usually followed earlier expeditions into the urban jungle. A curate was often dispatched to open a mission prior to churchbuilding. Depending on the availability of finance, the time gap could be a long one. St. Michael's began as a mission in 1839. It was thirty years before the church was built. Some missions followed the setting up of Sunday schools. This happened at Billinge in 1846. Other missions failed as money ran out before churchbuilding materialised. Such an attempt was the short lived mission near the canal attached to Bottomgate school. Opened in 1845, it was forced to close in 1847 through lack of finance. St. Matthew's, built 1884–86, was yet another church that started as an initially shortlived mission. The first mission room in Oxford Street, comprising three cottages knocked into one, was abandoned in 1874 due to a lack of funds. It was re-opened in 1880 using the new day school building, pending the completion of the new church.

The spread of the Presbyterian church followed a similar pattern to the Church of England. A mission, based on the Sunday school, was opened in 1882 on Whalley Range to be followed nineteen years later by the new church. Nonconformist chapels also often had humble and chequered beginnings. The congregation of Harwood Street chapel had their first services in a cottage in 1860 before moving to a warehouse in 1864. The chapel itself was built in 1875. Altom Street chapel, built in 1901, had its origins in a cottage in 1872. Services carried on in 1874 at the new school built in Kendal Street before transferring to the new chapel. Haslingden

Road chapel, built in 1866, started in a cottage in Kemp Street alongside a Sunday school. The owner hawked peas for a living. Alice Street chapel, opened in 1880, had its origins in Stout Street in the first ragged school in Blackburn. Then it moved to a house in Dale Street and from there to a mill in Pearson Street.

This peripatetic existence of many churches and chapels is indicative of another major factor leading to building delays: lack of finance. It is here that Blackburn's major employers once again enter the picture. Some saw helping to build places of worship as part of their civic duty. Many others did not. As the proportion of Church of England adherents to Nonconformists entering business was equal in relation to their respective numbers in the community, then it will be seen that the Anglican church had a possible financial edge. But even the Nonconformists had a fair number of employers with deep pockets. This is not true of the Roman Catholic community who supplied very few employers.

Money for most churches and chapels was raised by public subscription, and local employers sometimes contributed large sums. The Audley Range Congregational church of 1890 was indebted to Eli Heyworth for a £1,000

Paradise United Methodist Free Chapel, built in 1836 and demolished in 1871. Nonconformism was late in gaining a foothold in Blackburn and during the nineteenth century never attained the dominant position that it did in other northern industrial towns. Blackburn remained a Church of England enclave. *Courtesy of Blackburn Library*

donation, though the church was still in debt to the tune of £1,250 in 1902. Earlier, Joseph Eccles had been the main benefactor of Mill Hill Congregational Church. The Church of England also benefited from such generosity. The building of St. Luke's in 1876 was aided by money from Daniel Thwaites and Joseph Harrison, whilst St. Phillip's was built by the Dugdales for themselves and their workforce in the 1880s.

Such generosity, however, was not as widespread as might be expected or as popular belief might have us believe. Signs of parsimony among the employer class could already be seen in the 1820s when the building of the new parish church was held up due to lack of funds. When the Rev. Whittaker wanted a church built in the industrial suburbs of Grimshaw Park and Nova Scotia it was the lack of finance that once again hindered progress. Though first planned in 1839 and land was donated for the purpose by Joseph Feilden in 1840, Christ Church was not finally built until 1857–59. The reason was the lack of donations from local millowners. The Hopwood millowning family with 2,600 looms, 140,000 spindles and 2,500 workers in the vicinity finally put up three-quarters of the cost of the church. It appears, however, that this was mainly due to the persistence of Robert Hopwood's sister, who donated part of her own fortune. It was not only civic architecture that suffered from a lack of interest from the town's elite but religious as well.

This was especially so in certain quarters of Blackburn. Many other areas of the town were not as fortunate in finding benefactors, even belated ones. St. Thomas in the poor Bottomgate area of Blackburn was financed entirely by a door to door appeal to the local community. It took ten years to raise the necessary monies. The church opened in 1865. St. Matthew's at Higher Audley faced similar difficulties. Here the only major employer in the area was a Nonconformist. In 1884 £700 was collected in a house to house appeal and the remainder raised with great difficulty, mainly through the taking up of numerous small loans from local people. The church was still £1,200 in debt two years after it was built. St. Silas, consecrated in 1900 and situated in the relatively affluent area of Billinge and Mile End, also had no major benefactors. Once again the local community shared the burden, though they obviously found it easier to raise the money than did parishes in working-class districts. Employer generosity in financing churchbuilding in Blackburn was not as widespread as might be thought in an age of middle-class public piety and regular church attendance. Perhaps Blackburn businessmen preferred to see returns on capital in this life rather than the next.

Employers certainly saw religion as an important element holding together the fabric of society and one that could be influential in many ways. Chapter 6 shows how religion and elementary education, including

These ceiling panels in Holy Trinity Church were each painted with the recently purchased coats of arms of the leading families of the town who donated monies towards the cost of the building of this church in the 1840s. This is another example of the way the town's newly risen elite strove for social acceptance in their new position. *Photo by Ian Beesley with permission of the Redundant Churches Commission*

Sunday schools, were greatly intertwined in Blackburn and how deeply employers involved themselves in this. Yet again there is little evidence of widespread financial involvement by employers, though they certainly favoured the movement.

The first Sunday school in Blackburn was opened in 1786 by the Church of England. By 1824 C. of E. Sunday schools catered for 1,100 children, Nonconformist schools a surprisingly large 1,276 and Catholic schools 100. Fifty years later the figures were 9,500, 8,000 and 3,500 respectively. When all teachers and helpers are taken into consideration it is estimated that out of a population of 80,000 in 1875, 21,000 had Sunday school connections. As was seen in Chapter 6, employers encouraged this. It appears that there is some truth in the claim that mill salesmen, managers and overlookers owed their jobs as much to their diligence in attending church and chapel and being involved in Sunday schools, as to their application to their work.[4] Certainly a section of the working classes saw church attendance and participating in church or chapel activities as a vehicle for attaining respectability.

One influence that employers saw religion having on their workforces, and one that they encouraged, was that of a civilising one. Religion was seen as a tool of social control, a means of 'reforming the manners and morals of the lower orders'.[5] Christian doctrine, particularly as expressed through the Church of England, upheld the pattern of society and the belief that everyone had their place. It inculcated respect for rank and property and encouraged everyone to be content with their lot. So important did employers see church attendance by their workers that in 1834 they made Tuesday payday, believing drunkenness and hangovers or a combination of both the reason for low working-class attendance at Sunday worship. But this change merely led to absenteeism and low productivity on Wednesdays. The experiment was soon ended. Production came before church attendance in order of priority.

The churches certainly did their best to improve the social habits of the working classes. At St. Phillip's there was a bowling green and tennis courts. Church institutes offered a wide variety of leisure pursuits. St. Luke's institute in Dickinson Street offered a billiard hall and reading and refreshment rooms. In addition rambles, field days and picnics were organised. At St. Matthew's the range of clubs and societies included a burial society, temperance society, bookclub, savings and holiday clubs, cricket and football teams, cookery and dressmaking classes and a scripture union. Not all attempts were successful. It was claimed that by the 1860s attempts to make church institutes social and educational centres for the working classes had failed. From that point on most aimed at the middle-class youth.[6]

Organised religion certainly reflected the divisions caused by social class. This was especially so in the Church of England. Employers who helped to build some of the churches near their mills did not necessarily feel that they had constantly to attend them. Many split their attendance between it and one near where they lived. Large Tory employers in the early part of the nineteenth century used St. John's in the centre of the town. All the major families had their family vaults there. As the middle-class suburbs to the north west grew, the Tory elite moved not only their houses but their church. For the largest employers St. James at the top of Shear Brow or St. Silas on Preston New Road were frequented. For the middling Tory employers St. Peter's and St. Paul's were popular. Even Congregationalist employers had their preferences. The largest tended to use the Old Chapel Street and James Street churches.

Inside the churches yet more dividing lines were seen. Many pews were rented, some even purchased. Churchgoing was not necessarily free. At All Saints church only half of the 860 seats were free. The very poor of the area were even discouraged from attending at all. 'For those who are too poorly clad to come to church,' a cottage in Bolton Road at first sufficed, and then after 1888 a mission room was opened for them at the local ragged school.[7] Holy Trinity church had most of their free sittings in the gallery presumably in the belief that smells tend to rise rather than descend. St. Peter's had 700 rented pews whilst at Christ church less than half of the seats were free. The vicar defended this by claiming that 'our operatives are prepared to pay rather than be penned up in "free seats" as if paupers'.[8]

The best example of how congregations were so carefully separated can be seen by the experience of those who attended James Street Congregationalist church as late as the Edwardian period. To rent the front pews cost £10 p.a. Here were found the millowning families of the Birtwistle's and the Dugdale's. Behind them, paying slightly less, came the mill managers, travellers and salesmen. Further back still at £3 p.a. sat the overlookers, clothlookers and local shopkeepers. In the rear rented pews at a mere 8/- (40p) p.a. came the middle-class widows. The working classes, mainly skilled men and their families, sat at the back of the church in the free seats.[9]

Such divisions were long lasting and were the cause of resentment amongst many of the so-called lower orders. There had been trouble over pew payments back in 1839, during the early Chartist period, when a large number of people marched to a service at the parish church, sat in the reserved pews and refused to move. They asked the vicar to give a sermon based on the text 'Go to now ye rich, weep and howl for the miseries that are coming to you'. It had no effect. The meek failed to inherit, and rented pews persisted into the twentieth century. At St. Silas church the pew rental system was ended as recently as 1982.[10]

Perhaps such treatment was one explanation why many of the working classes were not churchgoers, even though most had attended church schools or Sunday schools or both. When the Rev. Whittaker came to Blackburn in 1821, church attendance was at a low ebb. St. Mary's was being rebuilt whilst St. John's was barely one-third full and the newly built St. Peter's saw only an average of fifty on a Sunday. Church attendance had picked up by the time of the religious census in 1851. Because of the way the census was carried out it is difficult to extract accurate figures. The census does show that in Blackburn 18,240 attendances at church or chapel services were recorded that day out of a total population of 46,536. How many were the same people attending two services is not known. What is

The gallery in Holy Trinity Church where the poor sat safely removed from the sight of their 'betters' who could afford to pay for their pews in the main body of the church. *Photo by Ian Beesley with permission of the Redundant Churches Commission*

almost certain is that many were from the middle classes for whom, by then, churchgoing was an expected and integral part of the social round. If it is presumed that the bulk of Blackburn's middle class did attend church that day then it follows that only 10–15% of the working classes did.

Evidence seems to suggest that attendances then declined as the century progressed. Only 20% of Blackburn's population were still churchgoers by 1880.[11] A 1904 survey in the Christ Church parish shows only 1,550 out of a possible 11,200 attended church on Sundays, just 14%.[12]

The fact that many of the working classes failed to go to church does not mean that they were irreligious, though some undoubtedly were. Dr. Rushton, the new vicar of St. Mary's in the 1850s, was pelted with a shower of sods on his first visit to the Nova Scotia and Grimshaw Park area. As children walked to St. Peter's from Bank Top to be confirmed in 1857 they had to run a gauntlet of 'jibes and scoffs of ungodly neighbours'.[13] But most of the working classes, though never seen in church, would still describe

Blackburn Cemetery. Even in death, class divided the people of Blackburn. The paupers had their own unmarked section of the cemetery but the remainder paid vastly differing amounts for their burial plots. In 1870 the cost of similar sized plots varied from £1 to £9. The amount depended on the plot's position in relation to the main entrances to the three chapels of rest – Church of England, Nonconformist and Roman Catholic. In Blackburn the hymn 'Nearer my God to Thee' had financial overtones. Though some of the elite provided the departed with large memorials and some, as above, with mildly exotic ones, compared to other northern cemeteries Blackburn funeral architecture is muted. Even in death the town's elite were parsimonious as regards funding the arts.

Photo by Ian Beesley

themselves as Church of England, as evidenced by the cold light of marriage and burial records and the hot flush of parliamentary and street demonstrations.

Politics, church and chapel were never far apart throughout nineteenth-century Blackburn. The close connection between religion and voting habits and the use made of this by the town's elite has already been seen in Chapter 3. Suffice it to note here the make up of the town council in 1861/2. Of the 54 councillors, six described themselves as Independent. Of the 30 Tories, all belonged to the Church of England. Of the eighteen

Liberals only three were Anglicans; two were Catholics and the remaining thirteen Nonconformists. The Catholics at this time tended to support the Liberal party in Blackburn. This loyalty became strained over the voluntary school issue following Forster's education act of 1870. By the end of the century this religious argument meant that many Catholics had switched their support to the Conservatives.

As early as the 1830s and the days of the Political Union agitating for parliamentary reform through to the decline of Chartism in the 1840s, radicalism and the chapel were connected. The Wesleyan chapel in particular was used for many political meetings; George Meikle and Richard Marsden, Blackburn's leading chartists, were Wesleyans. On the other religious flank it was not surprising that in 1838 the membership of the Operatives Conservative Association that met on Tuesday evenings was virtually the same as that of the Protestant society that met on a Thursday.

After 1868, when Gladstone planned and carried out the disestablishment of the Church of Ireland and then formed school boards, part of whose job was to ensure non-denominational religious teaching in the schools under their control, the cry 'Church in Danger' became a rallying call for all Conservatives. Political rallies and demonstrations were given church blessing. It is not surprising, therefore, that many parades in Blackburn ended up in violent incursions into the Catholic Irish quarter of the town with resultant mayhem.

Church encouragement of such events was not lukewarm. 'If anything unusually wicked or fallacious was said, it was ten to one it was said by a clergyman in Blackburn.'[14] It has to be borne in mind that John Morley, who exclaimed this, was a Liberal, but that cannot be said of *The Times* which stated of Blackburn's Rev. Wescoe, 'He is not a Conservative but simply a lunatic'.[15] As a result of such encouragement, loyalty to church or chapel by the working classes in Blackburn in the second half of the century was more akin to the present day worship of local football teams, and they wore their colours with defiant pride.

Even Sunday schools were not immune. The annual Whitsun march was often just an excuse to show off sectarian strength. Many Sunday schools took part in the Reform demonstrations of 1866, and in 1869 they joined in the street battles over the issue of Irish Church disestablishment. In the years that followed, Sunday school students were often present at Orange Order meetings.

But such a grip on the populace depends upon religious and political issues coinciding. This grew less and less in the years up to 1914. Class issues began to take their place, and church and chapel receded in the minds of the great majority of Blackburn's inhabitants.

After a fumbled beginning, organised religion certainly attempted to adapt itself to urbanisation. The Church of England had a head start in Blackburn and managed to keep it; sometimes with the help of energetic churchmen; sometimes with the self-interested help of the employer class; and sometimes even with the help of the clog. The battle for the souls of a rapidly growing population though was never won. Religion, at one point or other, certainly touched upon the lives of nearly all in Blackburn. It failed, however, to hold on to the majority of them, especially the working classes. In spite of all the new chapels and all the fresh towers and spires that rose to join the hundreds of factory chimneys, in the final analysis urbanisation in Blackburn weakened the grip of organised religion.

REFERENCES

1. Quoted in W.A. Abram, *A History of Blackburn*, J.G. & J. Toulmin, Blackburn, 1877.
2. *Wesleyanism in Blackburn; Bazaar Booklet*, Blackburn, 1913.
3. Quoted in B. Lewis, *Life in a Cotton Town: Blackburn 1818–1848*, Carnegie Press, Preston, 1985, pp.56–7.
4. P. Joyce, *Work, Society and Politics*, Harvester Press, London, 1980.
5. *Blackburn Standard*, 2 July 1823.
6. *Blackburn Standard*, 16 December 1868.
7. *All Saints Church Bazaar Booklet*, Blackburn, 1900.
8. *Christ Church Jubilee Handbook*, Blackburn, 1907.
9. *James Street Congregational Church Bazaar Booklet*.
10. Annual Report of the Parochial Church Council, St. Silas Church, 1982. My thanks to Robin Whalley for bringing this to my attention.
11. Rev. Hignett in *Blackburn Standard*, 6 December 1880.
12. *Christ Church Handbook*.
13. *St. Luke's Centenary Pamphlet*, Blackburn, 1976.
14. *Blackburn Times*, 17 October 1868.
15. Quoted in *Blackburn Times*, 17 October 1868.

9

The Great War and after, 1914–1939

In 1914, and in the coming years, many of the men of Blackburn went off to fight. Some never came back. Those that did returned to a town enjoying a post-war boom that would prove sadly shortlived. The Great War may not have been the war to end all wars that so many fervently hoped it would be, but it did deal the death blow to Britain's dominance of the cotton industry. As for Blackburn, for a town that lived and breathed cotton, the sudden decline of the mills was more than just painful. In the interwar years Blackburn too exhibited signs of dying. With the demise of the town's cotton industry the dominance of 'King Cotton' over the town's elite, its politics and virtually every other aspect of urban life was severely shaken. Much of cotton's legacy, however, would prove difficult to shed quickly.

As elsewhere in Britain, the declaration of war in August 1914 was greeted with enthusiasm and fervent patriotism. One of the few exceptions was Philip Snowden, one of the town's two MPs, who steadfastly opposed the war. He was to feel the electorate's backlash at the next election. By the end of September, in addition to the local territorials, 3,510 Blackburn men had already volunteered to serve in the regular army. Perhaps indicative of the state of health of the average Blackburn man, 18% were deemed unfit to serve.[1] But of those that did go, and continued to go, four won the Victoria Cross.

The war also affected the local economy. Whilst the men patriotically went off to serve 'King and Country', the women left behind found themselves involved more and more in the running of the local economy. Unlike in other towns and cities in the United Kingdom, this was not a new experience for many of them, though the diversity of jobs available was. As will shortly be seen, women became employed on the town's trams for the first time. In addition 300 women also served with the local police in the Women's Police Aid Detachment.[2] Even with such opportunities opening up, however, life on the Home Front became progressively harder. Though employment was easily come by as production for the war effort increased in tempo and a rise in real wages was experienced, food became dearer when imports declined as shipping space was more and more needed for war materials. Finally rationing was introduced. The Local Food Control Committee set up headquarters in Richmond Terrace in September 1917 and oversaw the organisation of this.[3]

When peace finally came in November 1918 the townspeople rejoiced and looked forward to the return of their loved ones and a better life than the one they had led back in 1913. Aspirations had grown and families dreamed of 'a land fit for heroes'. It was not to be. Not only would the diversification of jobs for women be shortlived but the war would lead to the decline of the cotton industry on which the town's economy was based.

The collapse of the cotton industry was spectacular. Discerning eyes had seen the danger signals before 1914, but the war accelerated the decline so much that Lancashire was totally unprepared for what happened in the interwar period. National cotton exports were especially hard hit. Exports of cotton cloth to the U.S.A. fell from 163 million yards in 1924 to eleven million in 1931. Exports to Brazil over the same period fell from 63.5 million yards to three million. But it was the dramatic fall in the export of the plain grey cloth to India in which Blackburn's mills specialised that hurt this town the most. In 1913 India annually imported 3,000 million yards of cotton cloth. In the entire interwar period that country rarely purchased more than 1,500 million yards in any one year, and the amount had fallen below 500 million yards by 1936 and never recovered.

Cut off from Blackburn's cotton cloth during the war years of 1914–1918, India had rapidly expanded her own cotton industry. In 1913 it was already producing 1,105 million yards of cloth annually. By 1931 it had more than doubled that output to 2,561 million yards and was still growing. Ironically, it was then helped by the purchase of second-hand looms from Blackburn's mills as, one by one, they closed down. In addition, the town's Technical College, with a world-wide reputation for high quality textile courses, trained overseas students from competitor countries. Blackburn thus accelerated her own decline.

The fact that imported cotton cloth became a pawn in Indian nationalist politics also did not help. Gandhi called for a boycott of all imported cloth in 1921 in favour of Indian handwoven cloth. Nine years later in 1930, the Congress Party played the same boycott card.

Other factors also helped increase Blackburn's woes. The fall in the purchasing power of the Indian peasant was yet another reason as the worldwide fall in the price of primary products hit India's earnings. An unstable rate of exchange also failed to help. In April 1919 one rupee equalled 1/6d (7.5p); by February 1920 it was 2/10d (14p); by March 1921 it was back to 1/3d (6p).

The raising of tariff barriers on imports to India also hurt. In March 1921 they increased 3.5% to 11%; in 1930 they rose to 15%; in March 1931 to 20%; and in October of the same year to 25%. This further protected and encouraged the growth of the domestic Indian cotton industry. When Gandhi was in Britain for political talks in 1931 he visited the Blackburn area. After being invited to see first hand the effect on the local mills of the loss of the Indian market, he explained:

> The poverty I have seen distresses me but compared to the poverty and pauperism of the starving millions of India, the poverty of Lancashire dwindles into insignificance.[4]

He may have had a valid point, but it was almost certainly lost at the time on Blackburn's unemployed.

But the final nail in the coffin of Blackburn's cotton industry, and the one that ensured that the lid remained forever closed, was the rise of Japan's cotton industry. In 1913 virtually all India's cotton cloth imports

This photograph was taken on Gandhi's visit to the area in 1931. It was hoped that a first hand look at the poverty caused by the local decline of cotton production, to a great extent brought about by the loss of the Indian market, would move him. It did, but not enough to help Blackburn.
Courtesy of Blackburn Library

came from Lancashire and most from Blackburn. By 1930 only 50% of cotton cloth imports into India were from Lancashire: the other 50% nearly all came from Japan. With a modern industry using the latest automatic looms, benefiting from an abundant supply of cheap labour, and a workforce prepared to work longer hours than their Lancashire counterparts, the price of Japanese cloth undercut Blackburn's by anything between 12.5% to 60%. To rub salt into the wound, Japan was also beginning to infiltrate Britain's domestic market.[5] Add to this the slow adoption by the industry of artificial fibres and it could be seen that Blackburn's textile ills had no cure.

The state of the town's weaving mills graphically illustrated the story. By 1918 Blackburn's 150 mills had 90,000 looms working. As the postwar boom evaporated 25,000 looms were stopped by October 1921. By that Christmas it was 40,000, and by February 1922 48,000. Though a slight recovery now took place, one third of all looms in the town still lay idle in April 1923.[6] The industry was never to recover. Between 1919 and May 1936, 79 mills closed down, 44 of them rendered forever inoperable as the machinery was either sold off or dismantled. Blackburn's industry had thus lost 26,116 looms for good, but that was still not enough. The rest were still half idle and no capital was available to invest in modern machinery.[7] By 1939 yet more mills had closed. The town's weaving industry had been severely reduced and its small spinning base almost totally eliminated.

If Blackburn were to survive then its economic base had to change. However, restructuring was not helped when Lancashire was not designated a development area under the Special Areas Act of 1934. This greatly hindered Blackburn in that it was not eligible for financial help in attracting new industry to the area. That Blackburn did not fall within a special area was even more inexplicable to local people since it certainly had comparable levels of unemployment to the four areas that were chosen: South Wales, West Cumberland, Durham and Tyneside and South West Scotland. The average unemployment rates for those regions in 1931 were 39%, 36.8%, 34.4% and 33.6% respectively. This compared to the 40.1% experienced for the Lancashire weaving district as a whole. By the first six months of 1936 the comparable rates were 44.4%, 36.4%, 27.6% and 22.9%. In Blackburn the rate was 27.2%. The reason given for not awarding special area status to the weaving district of Lancashire was that the county had to be judged as a whole, and parts of it contained industries that were not so hard hit, especially around the Manchester area.[8] The unfairness of this was partially recognised when, belatedly, under the Special Areas (Amendment) Act 1937, schedule 5 of the Act was extended to cover Blackburn and its immediate surrounding area. This allowed the Special Area Commissioner to grant loans to new companies prepared to settle in the town.

Blackburn Council had already made a start at attempting to encourage this. In 1935 an Industrial Development Sub-Committee had been set up to offer companies sites or buildings in the town at low rents or low purchase price.[9] With the aid of the Special Area Commissioner, yet more inducements could be offered. Some successes were forthcoming. A Czechoslovakian firm producing man-made fibres came to Blackburn in 1937; Griffin Mills were taken over by a German firm making slippers; whilst a French firm making fine fabrics was also enticed to the town. With a fresh European war on the horizon, a gas mask factory was opened in Garden Street that at first employed 360 women, whilst a Royal Ordnance Factory was promised by the Government on a site at Lower Darwen which would bring work for over 2,000 people.[10]

Blackburn's first industrial estate also opened in 1938 at Whitebirk on the north-eastern edge of the town. Mullards, owned by Philips of Mitcham, was the first firm on the site, manufacturing radio valves and related products. Meanwhile, some of the town's own industries, outside of cotton, began to prosper.

British Northrop Loom Co. Limited was formed in 1902 by William Livesey of Greenbank Ironworks along with some others. This firm purchased the rights from the U.S.A to the new automatic loom recently invented by J.H. Northrop. Within three years it was manufacturing the loom in Blackburn at the Greenbank Ironworks. Two years later in 1907 the first Northrop building was erected which, by 1914, employed 220 men. During the interwar years, as the cotton industry declined in Blackburn and the rest of Lancashire, this firm supplied the nascent industries of South America and the Far East. In 1929–1931 their success resulted in major extensions to the factory being built along Philips Road, next door to the future Whitebirk industrial estate.[11]

The town's brewers also survived: Daniel Thwaites and Co.'s Star brewery at Eanam, Dutton and Co.'s Salford brewery, and the Lion brewery at Little Harwood. This last one, owned by Nuttall and Co. until 1924, was taken over by Matthew Brown and Co. of Preston who then transferred their entire brewing operation to Blackburn, extending and modernising their premises there in the 1930s.[12]

Cotton, however, still remained Blackburn's largest industry during the interwar years. Most workers were still dependent for employment on that sector. Out of a total working population of 75,202 in 1921, 35,700 were employed in the textile trade.[13] This meant that any decline within the cotton industry affected the town's levels of unemployment. By the 1930s these were consistently high.

Table 1   Unemployment in the 1930s

Year	% of insured unemployed [14]
1929	14.5
1930	41.8
1931	47.0
1932	35.1
1936	28.8
1937	21.5
1938	31.4

The worst monthly figure was in June ,1930 when unemployment reached 51.8%.

But these figures, bad as they are, do not tell the entire story for they hide short-time working and underemployment which occurred when weavers were given fewer looms to work. Since weavers were paid by the piece, this meant a reduced income, and these workers were not eligible for unemployment benefit. Underemployment was estimated to affect 40% of the workforce in 1935, and though this had fallen to 21% in 1936, it still meant that even in that year of recovery, almost 50% of the town's total workforce were either unemployed or underemployed. Such figures also hide the extent of long-tern unemployment. In a trade like weaving where employability depended on having the 'knack' of operating four looms or more at maximum efficiency, being unemployed for more than twelve months often meant that a person was deemed unemployable by mill managers due to loss of skills.[15]

The effect on wages of all this was to depress them. In an industry where earnings were based on piece rates, and at a time when local agreements were being constantly and successfully flouted by employers, accurate figures are difficult to come by. In nearby Burnley, four-loom weavers in 1922 averaged £2-6s-0d (£2.30) per week.[16] This would have been somewhat lower than that earned in the boom period 1920–21. It would have been little different in Blackburn. But by 1936 a four-loom weaver in Blackburn only earned £1-11s-6d (£1.58).[17] Those underemployed on fewer than four looms would earn even less.

The plight of the unemployed was at least alleviated by unemployment insurance. The original Act of 1911 was extended in the 1920s to cover most manual workers. In addition the period of benefit was increased and additional benefits were added for dependants. This took some of the pressure off the local Poor Law and the Board of Guardians in the 1920s and the Public Assistance Committees in the 1930s. Benefits, however, were not high. In 1936 an unemployed single man would receive 17s (85p). If he had exhausted his period of insurance benefit then he would only receive a maximum of 15s (75p) unemployment assistance.[18]

One effect of high unemployment on Blackburn was a slow but accelerating decline in population. This was also partly due to a falling birth rate. Admittedly a comparatively low birth rate had always been a feature of the town due to the high incidence of working women outside the home. What really lay behind the fall was that a low birth rate was no longer compensated for by migration into Blackburn. Instead there was now an outward flow of migrants. The decade 1921–1931 saw a population fall of 6,529 from 129,400 in 1921 to 122,971 in 1931. This followed on the heels of a 3,652 fall in the previous decade. Matters got worse in the eight years prior to 1939. The previous migration rate of 3.7% for 1921–1931 rose to 6.9%. This, together with the excess of deaths over births, led to a net decline in Blackburn's population over the period 1931–1939 of 9%. Since it was mainly the young that tended to move away in search of employment, since they had fewer ties to restrain them, Blackburn also had a rapidly ageing population.[19]

High unemployment also affected the unions. The 'list', which stipulated agreed rates of pay for the job across the town's mills, collapsed as employers searched for ways of reducing costs. By July 1932 less than six of the town's mills still paid the agreed rates.[20] This abandonment of collective agreements was resisted by the unions, and industrial action occurred especially in the early 1930s and was epitomised by the 'Great Strike' of 1932. However, mass blacklegging, or 'knobsticking' as it was locally called, brought defeat after defeat. The main culprits were women.[21] Why they consistently failed to support their union is unclear. Possibly it was because they were less politically motivated than men. Perhaps it was partly that they needed the stamps to qualify for unemployment benefit. Certainly the Unemployment Insurance (Anomalies) Regulations of 1931 had made it much more difficult for married women to claim benefit. Or perhaps it was because many women put their families, and especially their children, before their union or their fellow workers.

Whatever their motive, such people were expelled from their union, others left as they became unemployed and found it difficult to keep up the payment of their weekly dues. The membership of the Blackburn Weavers Association fell 48.3% between 1929–1938. This dramatically hit their finances, and with the constant drain caused by the payment of strike pay, they found themselves in financial difficulties. In the four and a half years up to the summer of 1933 the textile unions in Blackburn had paid out £150,000 but only received an income of £107,000. As a result, they were forced to stop benefits to members who had never been given their jobs back after the 'Great Strike' of 1932.[22] A declining membership, dwindling finances and mass 'knobsticking' had increasingly weakened Blackburn's trade union movement throughout this period. What little militancy there had been, either at leadership or rank and file level, had soon evaporated.

Apathy, seen growing in the industrial sphere, was also reflected in the wider political arena. The National Unemployed Workers Movement (N.U.W.M.), formed in London in 1921 and basically a communist front organisation, though very active nationally was never very strong in Blackburn. It was often at crossed swords with the Blackburn Weavers Association and found little support for its attempts to highlight the plight of the unemployed. The N.U.W.M., like other organisations at this time, organised and helped co-ordinate hunger marches that walked the length and breadth of the country. Blackburn, however, remained relatively immune from them. Admittedly this was partly due to its geographical isolation, but even marches that started from the town were poorly supported. The largest march the town saw was one against the introduction and local administration of the Means Test. This was organised in 1932 with the destination being the headquarters of the Public Assistance Committee at Preston. Less than 1,000 took part.[23] The town saw occasional 'fierce battles' and police baton charges, but they were only precipitated by the actions of a small core of militants.[24]

The political right fared no better. The British Union of Fascists (B.U.F.), founded in 1932 by Sir Oswald Mosley, mistakenly chose Blackburn to be the starting point of their Lancashire recruiting campaign in January 1935.[25] With its high unemployment levels, and its traditional high level of working-class Conservative voting, the town seemed fertile ground. Mosley himself, at the head of his blackshirts, came to speak. The meeting ended early amidst fighting.[26] But this violence can give the wrong impression. Apart from that day's scuffles, the only other overt opposition to the B.U.F. were a few desultory letters to the local newspaper. It was political apathy that ensured minimal support for Mosley and his ilk. Blackburn's population remained impervious to political extremism whether it emanated from the far left or far right.

The town's General Election results show this same tendency toward political conservatism. Philip Snowden was the first victim of this. He had been the town's Member of Parliament since 1906 but found himself ejected in 1918 for daring to speak out against the war. Labour candidates never got elected again until 1929. By 1931 they had once more disappeared. Conservatives, as they had done in the nineteenth century, dominated the town's two seats at Westminster. A Coalition Liberal did sit

Philip Snowden was MP for Blackburn from 1906 to 1918 and was the first really to make a strong indentation into the Conservative monopoly of the town's two Westminster seats. A socialist, he stuck to his principles in 1914 and refused to support the war. As a result Philip Snowden joined the 'Great Fallen' in 1918 when Blackburn's patriotic electorate threw him over in that year's General Election. He successfully departed for pastures new and became the Chancellor of the Exchequer in the first two Labour Governments of 1924 and 1929–31.

Courtesy of Blackburn Library

Table 2   Social make-up of the Council [27]

	Aldermen	Councillors
1912–1913		
Cotton/Gentlemen	6	8
Other Manufacturers	1	5
Professional Middle class	5	9
Shopocracy	1	13
Working Class and Trade Union Representatives	1	6
1920–1921		
Cotton/Gentlemen	7	9
Other Manufacturers	1	2
Professional Middle Class	1	10
Shopocracy	1	8
Working Class and Trade Union Representatives	1	13
1930–1931		
Cotton/Gentlemen	3	2
Other Manufacturers	1	0
Professional Middle Class	2	6
Shopocracy	3	15
Working Class and Trade Union Representatives	5	18
1939–1940		
Cotton/Gentlemen	3	1
Other Manufacturers	0	2
Professional Middle Class	4	8
Shopocracy	4	14
Working Class and Trade Union Representatives	3	16

from 1918 to 1922, a National Liberal from 1922 to 1923, and a Liberal from 1923 to 1929, but only by running in agreed harness with a Conservative. Once this cosy agreement broke down, with the exception of 1929–1931, two Conservatives represented Blackburn right through to 1945. The Liberal Party even failed to put up candidates in the 1930s.

One section of the political arena, however, that did alter dramatically was the social make-up of the town council. A new political leadership, based on the shopocracy and the skilled working class, rapidly replaced that based on the cotton elite. As Chapter 3 showed, the beginnings of this can be discerned in the years leading up to 1914. The decade that followed peace in 1918, however, saw the power of the cotton manufacturers, and of those manufacturers in related industries, eclipsed on the town council. Their power declined with their industry (see Table 2). Though cotton kept a small foothold amongst the self-electing Aldermen, on the main council their grip was virtually eliminated. The demise of cotton's power may have been even more dramatic than the above table suggests since the term 'Gentleman' has been taken in its main nineteenth-century usage to mean a retired mill owner. This may not have been the case in the twentieth century. The only group to have remained unaffected in terms of their share of power was the professional middle class.

Yet another aspect of nineteenth-century Blackburn that changed in the interwar years was the employment position of women. Women had originally entered cotton textiles because their labour, and that of their children, was cheaper than that of men, and men at that time could still find employment elsewhere, especially in handloom weaving. Though men moved into the mills with the advent of the power loom, wage levels remained low compared to spinning and both men and women received the same piece rates. This low wage meant that both husband and wife often had to work in order to support a family. This situation had not changed by 1921. In this year, out of a total town population of 129,400, 33,466 women and girls over the age of twelve were employed outside the home. Nearly as many women had paid employment as men, 45% of the borough's workforce being female. And 75% of these worked in the mills. Marriage made little difference. Of the 33,466 working girls and women, 11,500 were married and 9,600 of these were employed in textiles.[28] A working wife had been a longstanding and acceptable part of family life in Blackburn.

Rising and long-term unemployment changed this. Women were to bear the brunt of a deep-seated change in the town's industrial base. In 1930 34.4% of the unemployed were men who had worked in textiles compared to 56.1% women. The gap had not much altered by 1938 when the figures were 25.4% and 38.5% respectively. Since these figures are based on calculations made from the Local Unemployment Index then it is more than possible that the gap was greater, since many women may no longer have registered as unemployed having given up the hope of paid employment and often no longer being eligible to claim unemployment benefit.[29]

Older women were the most severely hit. In 1931 38.3% of unemployed women were between the ages of 18–34, whilst 50.4% were aged 35 or over. The difference was even more pronounced with long-term unemployment. Women over 45 were eleven times more likely to be unemployed for more than twelve months than those under 25. Women applicants under 30 to the Unemployment Assistance Board made up only 6.8% of the total, whilst 35.7% were between 30–45 and 64.3% were over 45.[30]

Married women too were disproportionately discriminated against when it came to workers being laid off or in obtaining new jobs. In 1931 56% of married women were unemployed compared to 44% of single women. Married women were also more likely to be the long-term unemployed. There was no serious unemployment amongst young women in Blackburn in 1938 but there was still a steady increase in long-term unemployment for those over 24 who were more likely to be married.[31]

One reason for the high incidence of unemployment amongst women was a refusal by many to entertain the thought of any other job than in a factory or mill. Attempts to coerce unemployed mill girls to enter domestic service mainly failed because such work was seen as an inferior occupation. This antipathy to domestic service even brought opposition to taking seasonal posts as domestics in Blackpool and Southport or as canteen workers in army camps in the south.[32]

But the main reason was male chauvinism and the belief that a woman's rightful place was within the home. This was partly a product of the time and partly the resurfacing of a view that had lain dormant in the town due to the acknowledged need for a second wage. Since only one wage was now often possible the growing view was that it should be the man's. Such a view had always been prevalent outside of cotton weaving in Blackburn. Women had never been employed on the town's trams prior to 1914. By 1917, due to the conscription of men into the armed forces, there were twelve women drivers, 42 conductresses and two female ticket inspectors. All lost their jobs when peace came and the trams remained an all male enclave for the entire inter-war period.[33]

That society as a whole preferred to see women in the home, or at least in jobs deemed more suitable to their sex, can also be seen in the town during this period. The *Blackburn Times* publicly supported the idea that unemployed female weavers should become domestic servants and gave highly favourable reports of domestic service training centres in the town.

They also voiced the view that unemployment benefit for married women was a 'marriage subsidy or state dowry'.[34] The Pilgrim Trust held out the hope that the high unemployment rate amongst Blackburn's women would improve their skill in household management. They saw it as 'bad' or 'indifferent' when compared to the mining areas of South Wales where women traditionally did not work. The clubs opened up for unemployed women also show such an attitude in the type of activity that they encouraged. At the Y.W.C.A. dressmaking, millinery, cooking, first aid and shorthand and typing were the order of the day, whilst at the New Sunshine Club the main activities were the re-modelling and making of clothes.[35]

One aspect that may have marginally improved due to women's unemployment was the infant mortality rate in the town. But this, as in the nineteenth century, still remained far higher than the national average. The rate per 1,000 fell from 109 in 1921 to 80 in 1929 and 67 in 1938. But this should be compared to the national average of 83, 74 and 53 respectively. Only Stoke and Burnley, of towns with a population of over 100,000, matched Blackburn's figures, and they too had a tradition of large numbers of married women in work. The high incidence of mothers dying in childbirth was also inherited from the previous century. Between 1924 and 1929 this averaged 6.7 per thousand births.[36] Though the state of the mills, homes and the town in general played a part in this and in the high infant mortality rate, it was still mainly due to the fact that so many women still worked virtually to the end of their pregnancies, as they had done throughout the nineteenth century, in order not to lose too much in wages. The overall result on the health of the women of the town was plain to see. As Mary Hamilton, the borough's Labour Member of Parliament from 1929–1931, saw in 1924:

> At the first women's meeting I addressed, I was disappointed to see so few young faces, only realising later that many of these worn, haggard women were young, but looked, almost invariably, older than their age.[37]

The town also inherited a low birth rate from its past. In 1920 it was 20.1 per thousand compared to the national average of 25.4. It remained low throughout the interwar period despite fewer women working.[38]

The homes that more and more women were being forced to remain in were also a legacy of the nineteenth century and had altered little. Blackburn was:

> One of those typical Lancashire industrial centres .... Smoke darkens their skies; the little two-storey houses are set – no gardens – up and

down the cobbled streets; from the tiny 'lobby' you step straight to the roadway ... no trees, no grass, no playgrounds for the children.[39]

The Pilgrim Trust saw the town in the same grey light:

> The predominant impression which Blackburn leaves is that of grimness, unmitigated by any natural pleasantness, for the city is too large for much sense of the surrounding country to penetrate it. Everywhere is a forest of tall black chimneys, against a sky that seems always drab, everywhere cobbled streets, with the unrelieved black of the mill girls' overalls and the clatter of wooden clogs.[40]

But though the housing was unattractive it was in quite good condition, the overwhelming bulk of the houses being built in the second half of the nineteenth century. Many, therefore, were less than fifty years old. In a housing survey called for under the 1930 Housing Act, only 38 houses in

The drapery showroom in the Co-op Emporium in 1930 which offers a glimpse of shopping habits that have long since departed. The Co-op Emporium, after a facelift, is now the town library.
Courtesy of Blackburn Library

Blackburn were designated for slum clearance. In 1927 when Neville Chamberlain, the then Minister of Health, was shown the town's worst housing on a visit to Blackburn, he exclaimed; 'Is this all you have got to show me? It is not very bad. It is nothing like Manchester or Birmingham'.[41]

Overcrowding was not a problem either. Though little new housebuilding had taken place in the first two decades of the twentieth century, the fall in population meant that official overcrowding was only 3.9% in 1921 compared to the average of 9.6% for the whole of England and Wales.[42]

The continued fall in the town's population and the lack of house clearance schemes given the standard of the existing housing stock meant that the amount of housebuilding in the interwar years was not great. What little that did occur was mainly in the area of council housebuilding. 1,993 council houses were built between 1919 and 1939 at a cost of just over £1 million. This was mainly financed through Government subsidies under a number of Housing Acts. In contrast only £40,000 in such subsidies were paid to private housebuilders by 1934. Private housebuilding remained relatively stagnant up to 1939. The lack of a sizable middle class in the town allied to the lack of industrial growth meant that the typical middle-class suburbs of the interwar years, so common elsewhere, are largely missing in Blackburn. One important housing change that did start to come about had no effect on the townscape. This was the movement away from rented accommodation to owner occupation in the terraced streets. £135,000 was advanced to tenants under various Small Dwellings Acquisition Acts to enable them to buy the homes they lived in.[43]

The housing stock was also improved when the 9,253 remaining pail closets were virtually eliminated in 1922. In that year nearly all such modernised properties in the borough were converted onto the water closet system. This scheme was one of the public work schemes the town embarked on to create temporary work for the unemployed. Similarly, in 1924–1925 the town's 27,000 ashpits were replaced by galvanised iron dustbins.[44]

The new council estates, however, were the only major change in the built environment. Here too there was a link to the past. As mill colonies had helped shape the town in the early nineteenth century so now did council house colonies in the early twentieth century. The Addison Housing Act of 1919 imposed a duty on all local authorities to carry out a survey of the housing needs of their area. They were then obliged to submit plans to the Ministry of Health for the building of any housing shortfall. Impressed by the pre-war Garden City movement that had stressed the benefits of planned, low density housing incorporating trees, hedging and open spaces, the new Ministry insisted that houses, each with a garden, had to be of a certain size and standard and built no more than twelve to an acre on designed estates. This meant that virtually all such building would be on the outskirts of towns where land and greenery were more abundant. Blackburn chose three rural sites on the northern, eastern and south western boundaries of the town at Brownhill, Intack and Green Lane respectively. Green Lane and Intack were the first two to be built, but problems soon started to become apparent. Building on the outskirts of Blackburn allowed tenants to breathe fresh air and for housing to be less cramped, but what of the journey to work? The planning of the Brownhill estate took this problem on board. Built both sides of a new road, it was decided that this must be a dual carriageway with a tramway or light railway to be constructed on the central reservation. It never was.

Other problems also slowly came to light. Though extra land was purchased at Green Lane for a playing field and the Brownhill site plans incorporated a sixteen acre public park complete with bandstand and ornamental pool, not one of the new estates had a shop or public house. The Church of England was allowed to purchase land at Brownhill for a new parish church but that was all. The error made by virtually all local authorities, and one that would be repeated throughout the interwar period, of erecting isolated estates made up solely of housing units and lacking any sense of community, was also made in Blackburn.[45] Even the standard of municipal housing declined as the subsequent Chamberlain, Wheatley and Greenwood Housing Acts of 1923, 1924 and 1930 reduced the size and quality of the houses in order to build more homes more cheaply.

The relative dearth of new building, outside of council houses, experienced in Blackburn in the interwar period was even more pronounced as regards the provision of new schools. By 1936 Blackburn Education Committee, set up in 1903, had only built five new elementary schools and nearly all of these had been before 1914. As a result Victorian schools still dominated the town.

> The schools ... were in the main, old fashioned and badly planned: dark and draughty, with desks of the most uncomfortable type, and classrooms that were much too large.[46]

As for secondary schools, the authority failed to build even one before the Second World War. The only secondary education in the town was at Queen Elizabeth's Grammar School, at the Girls' High School, which still remained a private limited company until 1932, and at the two Roman Catholic schools, Notre Dame and St. Mary's College. The Church of England only opened St. Hilda's and St. Peter's in 1939.[47] Just as in Victorian times, it was felt that for the bulk of the children of Blackburn, a sound elementary education based on the three R's was quite adequate to

Council houses on Rosewood Avenue where it joins Briar Road in the mid 1930s. In depressed interwar Blackburn municipal housing was virtually the only new housing to be seen and there was not much of that. With a declining population, Victorian housing that was as yet in quite good condition and a small middle class, the housing stock was momentarily adequate for the town's needs and pocket.

Courtesy of Blackburn Library

fit them for a working life. It is not surprising that on the eve of the national abolition of half-time education in 1920, 30% of all boys and girls in the borough aged between 10–13 had employment and nearly 50% of those aged over twelve.[48]

It is also not surprising that the only new educational venture to be embarked upon in these years was the setting up of Juvenile Instruction Centres. The first was opened by Margaret Bondfield, the Minister of Labour, in October 1930. They gave practical training to some of the unemployed youth of the town. The only other educational growth area in Blackburn was the Technical College which now had 4,000 full and part-time students. All followed mainly practical courses of instruction. The belief, held by the cotton masters of the nineteenth century, that education should be geared to the world of work and the needs of the local economy apparently still held good with the town's new elite. The lack of any pressure to alter the situation also seems to point to the fact that parents too still appeared to hold to their Victorian counterparts' view that schooling should end as early as possible so that a wage could be earned.

The demands of twentieth-century transport also failed to alter the built environment of Blackburn during these years, though they did alter life within the town. The peak year for passenger journeys on trams was 1921 when 18.25 million journeys were made, an average of 50,000 per day. The onset of unemployment, allied to the rise of motor transport, ensured that this peak would never be surpassed. The coming of motor transport also brought growing traffic congestion. Though traffic signals were introduced in 1932, the situation grew steadily worse, and it was the trams that were blamed. Slowly tracks were lifted. The Audley route was dismantled in 1935. Finally in 1938 the council took the decision to replace trams completely with motor buses within five years. The war intervened, but all tram services were ended by 1949.[49] But congestion or not, the town's street pattern hardly altered. Lack of money and the lack of any central redevelopment plan saw to that.

Leisure patterns did alter. This was partly due to changing tastes and partly due to economic conditions. The summer holiday weeks in 1921, shortly after industrial recession set in, saw train bookings at Blackburn down 66%. They never fully recovered throughout this period. Instead a great demand arose for day excursions. Those that still took a week's holiday in Blackpool or another local seaside resort, often returned twice during the holiday: once to sign on and once to draw benefit.[50]

Theatre going increased, ballroom dancing became the rage, and the age of the dream palace arrived with sixteen cinemas in the town by 1939. Spectator sports continued to grow in popularity, and on occasions over

160

Blackburn Rovers winning F. A. Cup team of 1928. Spectator sport was growing in popularity and Saturday afternoons in Blackburn was a time to see the Rovers. Up to 60,000 spectators crowded into Ewood Park to forget their troubles for a few hours. *Courtesy of Blackburn Library*

60,000 supporters crowded into Ewood Park to cheer on Blackburn Rovers football team. Expenditure on such leisure pursuits meant less money available for others, which helped to produce only 53 convictions for drunkenness in 1932, the lowest ever recorded.[51]

Horticulture also grew as a leisure pursuit. In 1928 the Society of Friends formed an allotments committee in collaboration with the National Allotments Society. The town council also got involved finding suitable land as part of a Government scheme to aid the unemployed. Such men got plots free for the first year and then received a rebate of 4/6d (22.5p) off the annual 10/- (50p) rent. The Blackburn Council of Social Services erected huts on eleven sites and provided cheap seed, fertiliser and tools. A Jubilee Club was opened to encourage boys of 14 to 18 in horticulture. As a result, by the summer of 1936, 1,300 plots had been taken up on twenty sites throughout Blackburn. The biggest, of 50 acres, was at Whitebirk. This town, it appears, had one sixth of all the allotments in Lancashire.[52]

Some things, however, did not alter and class still intruded into leisure pursuits. Blackburn Golf Club increased their annual subscription by 50%

in 1920 to three guineas, a sum that ensured that any working-class, or even lower middle-class, element was excluded.[53]

Physically, Blackburn in 1939 had altered little since 1914. Change was on the horizon as new firms began to settle in the town, but they did not yet provide enough employment opportunities to come anywhere near redressing the balance following the severe decline of cotton. The bulk of the population still lived in Victorian terraced housing, and the town's political leadership, though itself much changed, appeared to lack any ideas to alter the situation. The people too lacked vision. Most had not shaken off traditional nineteenth-century attitudes.

> They took the industrial employment of married women with young children, the high disease and mortality rates, the heavy incidence of deafness, the stunted stature of the men and women, the dirt and darkness and lack of grace of the town and its deficiency of amenities, for granted.[54]

If Blackburn were ever to prosper again this would have to change.

REFERENCES

1. *Blackburn Times*, 10 October 1914.
2. *Weekly Telegraph*, 29 October 1921.
3. 1st Annual Report of the Local Food Control Committee September 1918.
4. *Blackburn Times*, 3 October 1931.
5. R. Pope, 'The Unemployment Problem in N. E Lancashire 1920–1938', unpublished MLitt. thesis, University of Lancaster, 1974, pp.60–84.
6. Pope, 'Unemployment in N.E. Lancs', p.29.
7. *Blackburn Times*, 5 December 1936; Pope, 'Unemployment in N.E.Lancs', pp.378–9.
8. Pope, 'Unemployment in N.E. Lancs', pp.96–8.
9. Pope, 'Unemployment in N.E. Lancs', p.93.
10. *Blackburn Times*, 16 January 1937 and 15 October 1937.
11. M. Rothwell, *Industrial Heritage: A Guide to the Industrial Archaeology of Blackburn Part II Other Industries*, Hyndburn Local History Society, 1986.
12. Rothwell, *Industrial Heritage*.
13. Lancashire County Census, 1921.
14. Pope, 'Unemployment in N.E. Lancs', p.33.
15. Denise Martin, 'Women Without Work: Textile Weavers in North East Lancashire 1919–1939', unpublished MA dissertation, University of Lancaster, 1985; Pope 'Unemployment in N.E. Lancs', pp.54–9.
16. Pope, 'Unemployment in N.E. Lancs', pp.179–180.
17. E.M. Gray, *The Weavers Wage*, London, 1937, p.31.
18. S. Constantine, *Unemployment in Britain Between the Wars*, Longman, London, 1980, p.28.

19. Pope, 'Unemployment in N.E. Lancs', pp.199–203

20. *Blackburn Times*, 30 July 1932.

21. Pope, 'Unemployment in N.E. Lancs', pp.253–4.

22. *Blackburn Times*, 16 September 1933.

23. Pope, 'Unemployment in N.E.Lancs', pp. 272–283.

24. *Blackburn Times*, 9 June 1932.

25. For the full story of this episode see Brenda Crosby, 'The Lancashire Campaign of the British Union of Fascists 1934–35', unpublished MA dissertation, University of Lancaster, 1977.

26. *Blackburn Times*, 12 January 1935.

27. Based on occupational details listed in the *Blackburn Borough Council Handbooks* 1913–1940 in Blackburn Library Local History Collection.

28. Lancashire County Census 1921 and Martin, 'Women Without Work'.

29. Pope, 'Unemployment in N.E. Lancs', p.33.

30. Pope, 'Unemployment in N.E. Lancs', pp.44–8.

31. Martin, 'Women Without Work'.

32. Martin, 'Women Without Work'.

33. John Clay, 'The Tramways of Blackburn 1851–1949', unpublished BA dissertation, Lancashire Polytechnic, 1984.

34. *Blackburn Times*, 28 November 1931.

35. Pilgrim Trust, *Men Without Work*, Cambridge, 1938, pp.223, 282–5.

36. Blackburn County Borough Health Department Annual Reports 1921–1938.

37. M.A. Hamilton, *Remembering My Good Friends*, London, 1944, p.175.

38. Health Dept. Annual Reports.

39. Hamilton, *Remembering*, p.174.

40. Pilgrim Trust, *Men Without Work*, p.82.

41. Quoted in Historical Summary for City Status Bid 1934 (in Author's possession)

42. Lancashire County Census 1921.

43. Historical Summary for City Status Bid 1934.

44. Historical Summary for City Status Bid 1934; Pope 'Unemployment in N.E. Lancs', pp.16–17.

45. D. Beattie, 'The Origins, Implementation and Legacy of the Addison Housing Act 1919, with special reference to Lancashire', unpublished PhD thesis, University of Lancaster, 1986.

46. Hamilton, *Remembering*, p.175.

47. *Blackburn Centenary Souvenir*, Blackburn, 1951.

48. Health Dept. Annual Reports.

49. Clay, 'Tramways of Blackburn'.

50. Pope, 'Unemployment in N.E. Lancs', pp.193–4.

51. Chief Constable's Annual Reports 1932–1939, Blackburn Library Local History Collection.

52. *Blackburn Times*, 4 July 1936.

53. *History of Blackburn Golf Club*, 1954, Blackburn Library Local History Collection.

54. Hamilton, *Remembering*, p.175.

10

Blackburn
since 1939

Blackburn emerged from the Second World War virtually unscathed as regards bomb damage. Just as in the Wars of the Roses, the English Civil War and the Jacobite Rebellions, Blackburn was either too difficult to find or not strategically important enough when compared to other towns and cities. The Luftwaffe dropped only three bombs on Blackburn. The first fell at 1 a.m. on August 30th 1940. It landed on Bennington Street and failed to cause any casualties. The second landed in Ainsworth Street just before midnight the following day. This time two people were killed and eight injured. On the third occasion, in October 1940, two bombs fell harmlessly on land at Whitebirk between the power station and the gasworks. A handful of other bombs fell nearby, the nearest being two at Guide and another on the village of Mellor. That was the full extent of the local damage wreaked by the German airforce.[1]

The town was affected in other ways. Evacuee children from the Manchester area were found homes with Blackburn families, and the scrap metal campaign of the early war years saw the ornamental gates of Corporation Park disappear along with most of its boundary railings. The same happened at Queen's Park. In addition, the two Russian cannons, mementoes of the Crimean War that had stood proudly above Corporation Park, were also sacrificed.[2]

The war more profoundly affected Blackburn both in terms of its wartime economy and in its following peacetime economy. The gasmask factory in Garden Street more than doubled its number of employees, mostly women, to 1,000. The Royal Ordnance Factory, making mainly fuses for anti-aircraft shells, increased in size until it was employing 5,000 workers of whom 85% were women. Special day nurseries were opened in order for young mothers to work there. British Northrop turned from making automatic looms to producing aircraft components and machine tools, whilst Mullards mass produced valves for military electronic systems.[3]

When the war ended in 1945 the jobs did not all disappear. Production of munitions at the Royal Ordnance Factory was cut back but not ended.

In addition the factory took on other work to keep employment levels up. The workforce even turned their hands to producing alarm clock mechanisms. The outbreak of the Korean War in 1950 brought more work, and a decision was taken by the Ministry of Defence to retain the factory as part of Britain's peacetime defence strategy. Up to 3,000 workers, still mostly women, were employed there in 1980.[4] Mullards returned to a renewed involvement in television set manufacture. By 1970 the factory covered 46 acres in Blackburn and annually produced millions of transistors, valves and capacitors.[5] British Northrop returned to making automatic looms and employed 2,000 workers at its Daisyfield factory in 1953. As demand for looms declined in the postwar years the company diversified to produce earth moving machinery and even furniture.[6] Other Blackburn firms also expanded or developed in the postwar years. The Scapa Group, having started business in the 1920s in a disused skating rink, employed 1,000 workers by 1967 making felt for the paper making industry.[7] C. Walker & Sons Ltd at Guide became Great Britain's largest steel stock holder with an annual turnover of 180,000 tons in 1975 compared to 1,000 tons in 1956.[8]

But though the war accelerated the town's move from textiles to engineering and other forms of manufacture, Blackburn still remained shackled to its past. The borough's rapidly ageing nineteenth-century housing stock was in growing need of renewal. In addition, for all the industrial change of the pre-war and war years, the town was, to a great extent, wedded to the still declining industry of cotton. Postwar austerity did not help an early start to rectify such problems. Structural unemployment was to remain a concern, and it was to be the 1960s before the physical shape of Blackburn was to alter and the borough attempted to escape from the environmental prison of its past.

Blackburn's population decline continued after the end of the Second World War. The total population in 1951 was 111,218, a drop of 11,574 since the last census of 1931. By 1961 it had declined even further to 106,242 and by 1971 to 101,825, a figure last recorded in the mid 1870s. Since Blackburn joined with Darwen to form a new enlarged borough in 1974, comparative population statistics for the more recent past are more difficult to ascertain. The population of Blackburn town did rise to 106,501 by 1981, thanks to large scale immigration from Asia that will be discussed later in this chapter, but then it carried on falling again when such immigration slowed. Between 1981 and 1987, though there was a net gain of 2,600 through an excess of births over deaths, there was a loss of 8,300 through net out migration. This was the opposite to the experience of Lancashire as a whole which saw a population loss of 5,400 through natural change and a gain of 900 through net in migration.

This continuing population fall was reflected in the decline of cotton. Though 1948-1950 saw a short post-war boom in textiles, the slow decline of the industry continued. The 33,326 jobs in the town's cotton mills in 1931 had fallen to only 12,491 by 1957. By 1965 jobs within the industry had been reduced to 7,495, and by 1977 to 6,572. Decline then accelerated in the late 1970s and early 1980s. The 1981 census showed that only 3,404 workers were then employed in Blackburn's textile industry and each following year saw even fewer. The 50 mills of 1955 became the 30 of 1960. By 1967 four more had closed. By 1983 only five were left; a mere rump of a once proud and dominant industry.[9]

The switch to engineering soaked up many of the jobs that cotton shed. By 1951 this industry employed 8,178 workers compared to 4,010 in 1931. The town council also helped the restructuring of Blackburn's industrial base. They provided further industrial sites at Whitebirk, new ones at Roman Road in the 1960s, and yet more at Shadsworth in the 1970s. More recently, in addition to yet further land at Whitebirk in the shape of Glenfield Park, the council have provided new sites for small industrial units in inner town localities. This continued attempt to attract new industry to Blackburn, however, has not kept pace with the loss of jobs. These have not just been confined to cotton. Contraction of other large-scale employers has also been experienced. R.O.F. employees are now counted in their hundreds instead of their thousands, Mullards has slimmed down dramatically, and British Northrop is now closed. Blackburn, though, in terms of employment and the size of its working-class base, has remained disproportionately committed to manufacturing even within a manufacturing region, as figures for 1981 (Tables 1 and 2) show.[10]

The switch to new industries and to a new industrial base was not, however, quick enough nor complete enough to avoid high, prolonged, local unemployment levels. Blackburn's recent experience shows this. The unemployment rate in 1977 was 6.5%. By July 1980 it had risen to 9%, rising again to 15.3% in August 1982. It never fell below 15% until 1986 and was still at 14.1% in 1987. Though Lancashire as a whole experienced a rate above the national average throughout this period it was still consistently around 4% lower than in Blackburn. In 1981 the county figure was 10.4% against Blackburn's figure of 14.7%.[11]

Blackburn's other major inheritance from its past was a rapidly aging housing stock. Most houses had been built in the second half of the nineteenth century, and many lacked one or more of the basic amenities. There had been little systematic renewal before 1960 with the result that in 1961 40% of Blackburn's entire housing stock was without a fixed bath or bathroom and as many were without an indoor w.c. The town council now

Table 1   Socio-economic groups, 1981

	Blackburn	Lancashire
Employers, Professional and Managerial	11.4%	15.5%
Other Non-Manual	27.2%	30.7%
Skilled Manual	30.9%	27.4%
Semi-Skilled Manual	22.4%	19.7%
Unskilled and Manual	7.1%	5.5%
ʹOthers	1.1%	1.1%

Table 2   Employment by industry, 1981

	Blackburn	Lancashire
Agricultural	0.5%	2.2%
Energy and Water	1.4%	2.3%
Manufacturing	40.6%	32.8%
Construction	5.4%	6.2%
Distribution and Catering	18.9%	20.7%
Transport	5.6%	5.2%
Other Services	27.5%	30.6%

decided on a twenty-year programme to clear 11,285 Victorian houses in designated clearance areas by 1982 and to build 13,400 new homes. These were to rehouse those whose houses had been demolished and to cater for an overcrowding figure of 4.6%.[12]

The result of this ambitious urban renewal programme by 1970 was mixed. Demolition ran ahead of schedule. 6,281 houses were cleared by that date. However, 58% of the town's housing stock was still two-up two-down Victorian terraced housing of which 23.2% remained part of the council's slum clearance plan. 25.8% of all private households still had no fixed bath and 42.2% had no indoor w.c. This compared to figures of 13% and 18.7% for Lancashire as a whole and 12% and 15% for England and Wales. In addition only 4,605 new homes had been built. It was estimated that 8,795 more new housing units were needed in the next ten years, but this necessitated a higher building rate per annum than even the nation's new towns were achieving. To compound the problem the council's housing committee now proposed to bring forward the date for clearing the remaining 5,004 houses designated for demolition to 1978. In addition they added a further 750 properties to the programme.[13]

A totally unexpected public outcry in 1970 now engulfed the town. Those living in the clearance areas did not want their communities destroyed, to be scattered to houses on various council estates or to be placed in high rise blocks of flats. In addition, those on the council house waiting list did not relish the thought of remaining there for many years to come as those being rehoused continually took precedence over them. The full council was forced to turn down the housing committee's plan. That committee was now asked to plan the town's urban redevelopment strategy around improvement schemes, encouraging householders to apply for grants to renovate and modernise their homes whilst the council dealt with the surrounding environment.[14]

This approach met with some success. Households lacking at least one basic amenity, such as a ready supply of hot water, a bath or indoor w.c., were reduced by 1990 to 14% of the privately owned housing sector. But the difficulty was that as the years passed yet more of the housing stock deteriorated and became in need of improvement or renewal. In 1990, of the 40,000 privately owned houses in the borough, 22,500 had been built before 1919. Admittedly the borough now encompassed Darwen, but these

Ever since the 1960s Blackburn has witnessed an ongoing urban renewal programme: whilst many of the terraced and setted streets have disappeared, a considerable number still remain.   *Photo Ian Beesley*

169

figures still accurately reflect the problem faced by the original borough of Blackburn. Because of this, even though improvement schemes were being carried forward and even some demolition was taking place (452 house clearances were made in 1989–1990 alone), it was estimated that 8,000 homes, 20% of the private housing stock, were deemed in need of substantial repair work. In addition, 5,000 homes, or 12% of the private housing sector stock, were deemed unfit and in need of clearance.[15]

Though slum clearance and house improvement schemes were one way in which the town's housing problem was tackled, the building of council-owned properties was another. Plans for large scale council house building were laid as early as 1946 when land at Shadsworth, on the outskirts of the town, were purchased. Building began there in 1953, and by 1958 the estate of 1,200 houses was completed. Further estates were begun in the 1960s as council house building accelerated in order to rehouse those families displaced through the house clearance programme. Building was seen at Queen's Park, Roman Road, Larkhill, Audley and Millhill, and the estate at Green lane was enlarged. All were finished by the end of the 1970s. As the table below shows, there was a movement to house those tenants who only required one or two bedrooms in flats. These were mainly provided in the form of tower blocks.

Table 3   Council property in Blackburn[16]

		Pre 1945	1945–1964	1964–1981
1 Bedroom	House	0	0	0
	Flat	124	800	2,041
	Bungalow	64	67	302
2 Bedrooms	House	914	627	840
	Flat	35	713	1,133
	Bungalow	0	0	20
3 Bedrooms	House	1,148	2,223	2,253
	Flat	0	93	350
	Bungalow	0	0	5
4 Bedrooms	All	13	117	205
Total		2,298	4,640	7,149

This emphasis on council building meant that such property made up an ever increasing proportion of Blackburn's housing stock. In 1961 it was 18.3%; by 1981 it had risen to 31%. This compared to a figure of 19.3%

for Lancashire as a whole. Thanks to the right to buy system, introduced in the 1980s to allow tenants to purchase their home at a reduced price, the figure had been reduced to 25% by 1990.[17]

Most new council housing now takes place in small mixed housing schemes in conjunction with private enterprise. Switching away from large council estates on the outskirts of the town, small inner town developments are now the order of the day where council and private houses stand side by side. The Daisyfield area of Blackburn has just seen the completion of such a scheme.

Much of the private housebuilding in the Blackburn area, however, has taken place outside the borough boundaries. Though large estates were built at Lammack and Pleckgate, others were to be found at Cherry Tree, Feniscowles, Mellor and Wilpshire. This local migration partly explains the population decline and was the reverse of the short distance inward migration that Blackburn experienced in the nineteenth century.[18]

Blackburn council also embarked on a major redevelopment of the town centre. Before cotton became the town's lifeblood, Blackburn had been the main market town of East Lancashire. With the demise of cotton it was decided that Blackburn should reclaim its former position. In 1961 it was decided that a new, modern shopping complex should be built, one that segregated pedestrians from traffic, provided covered shopping areas with ample open spaces, and included ample car parking facilities. The council entered into a partnership with private industry, in the shape of the Laing Construction Group, to carry out a joint development. Since the site of the new shopping centre included the old market, this had to be moved as a prelude to construction.

A new market was built on a site between Penny Street, Salford and Ainsworth Street. Started in 1961 it was finished in 1964. The first phase of the shopping centre development could then begin. The old market, together with its distinctive clock tower, was demolished. On its site was erected the first part of a shopping precinct and a new tower block extension to the Town Hall.

The second phase, covering the area between Ainsworth Street and Victoria Street, was built between December 1969 and November 1971. Thirty-seven small shops and three large stores, the Co-op, Boots and Tesco, were opened as well as a large addition to Woolworths. The centre was in three tiers. The lower one was for servicing, the middle for shopping and the top for car parking. Due to the shape of the land it was possible to enter the shopping area at ground level from King William Street. The third and final phase, carried out between 1977 and 1980, covered the area between Church Street, Lord Street and Astley Gate. Amongst many other shops it provided two more large stores, Debenhams and W. H. Smith.[19]

A new market, followed by a new shopping centre built in three phases, were built in the 1960s and the 1970s. This attempt to revitalise the town centre and re-establish Blackburn as the market town for East Lancashire soon dated, as has the statue of the young mother in mini dress, shoulder bag and sandals. Some of the larger stores that were housed there in the beginning have since departed and have not been replaced.

Photo by Ian Beesley

Much of Blackburn's nineteenth-century town centre, including Thwaites Arcade, disappeared with this major redevelopment. There is no doubt that in the short term this venture was a success, attracting many shoppers to the town since it was one of the first in the north west. In the long term the benefits are questionable. Certainly, within the few years since it has been built it has become dated. Later shopping centres in other textile towns have learned to blend the old with the new, to link the buildings of the past with the needs of the present. Blackburn, in its rush to be first whilst trying to be rid of its past, severed most of those links. The result has been that one of the next major shopping developments, the Morrisons complex, tried to resurrect a past, so recently obliterated, by incorporating a modern version of the demolished clock tower in its design.

The demolition of old Blackburn did not end with the construction of the shopping precinct. The Telegraph Building disappeared to make way for Morrisons. The Palace Theatre, a larger version of the successfully restored Bradford Alhambra, was only recently demolished. The highly ornate Victorian Technical College nearly went the same way but was saved. As with housing, some attempts have recently been made to keep some parts of the past and blend them in with the present. The restoration of Georgian Richmond Terrace was highly successful and the Eanam Wharf project, part of a plan to revitalise the Leeds–Liverpool canal area for housing, industry and recreation, looks highly promising. For many areas of the town, however, it is too late.

One other physical change that Blackburn has witnessed recently is the transformation of the parish church of St. Mary's. A diocese centred on Blackburn was created in 1927 and a fund was started in order to transform the parish church into a cathedral. The original plan by the architect W.A. Forsyth was for the original parish church to form the nave, a new chancel to be built with a crypt below and a new central tower to be added. Money was not easily found, however, and therefore building was only started in 1938 and was then immediately halted by the outbreak of war. Building recommenced in the early 1950s. Both transepts and two bays of the chancel were completed in 1956, but then the money ran out. The original design was abandoned and, after the death of Forsyth, Lawrence King was appointed architect in 1961. The part of the chancel that was already built now became the new shortened chancel in a new plan. The original plan for the new central tower was scrapped. It was to be replaced by a cheaper lantern tower surmounted by a needle spire and cross. The Cathedral was finally completed in 1977 and re-consecrated that year by Princess Alexandra.[20] This episode evokes memories of public building in the nineteenth century and especially of the half completed cotton

The Eanam Wharf project is one of a number of ways in which the local council, in conjunction with the town's local business community, is attempting to revitalise parts of Blackburn and attract both people and industry back to the town.   *Photo by Ian Beesley*

exchange. Generous expenditure on public buildings has never been one of the town's fortes.

A spate of new school building was also planned for Blackburn after 1945.[21] Following the Butler Education Act of 1944 which made free secondary education compulsory up to the age of fifteen, Blackburn Education Committee drew up two plans. The first, in 1947, was a development plan for nursery, primary and secondary education within the borough. The second, in 1948, was to increase adult education by expanding the Technical College and by building community centres on the new housing estates. Implementation, however, was slow in occurring. The 1950s only saw two new primary schools built at Lammack and Longshaw, and it was 1958 before the first two new secondary schools were built at Witton Park and Shadsworth.

Education received its first of many shake-ups only in 1964. It was agreed that all pupils between the ages of 11–14 would attend a Junior

High School. They could then remain for one more year and leave at fifteen or transfer to one of the two Senior High Schools for two years further education. This plan was implemented in 1966 and ended in 1968. It was replaced by a second scheme based on five comprehensive schools, three of which would be 11–16 and two 11–18. Within a short time this too had altered and all became 11–18 schools.

All five comprehensive schools were in modern buildings and all five were on the periphery of the town: Shadsworth (1958), Witton Park (1958), which was an amalgamation of Witton Park Secondary School and the Girls' High School, Everton (1966), Billinge (1966) and Pleckgate (1968). Queen Elizabeth's Grammar School opted out of this re-organisation and became independent. Change again came in 1984 when all five comprehensives lost their sixth forms which were transferred to the Technical College which was now transformed into a Tertiary College.

It was at this point that Blackburn's past once again caught up with it. The influence of the churches on education in the nineteenth century meant that the Church of England and the Roman Catholic church had secondary schools in the borough. These voluntary-aided schools refused to join in the sixth form re-organisation. St. Mary's Roman Catholic Sixth Form College remained and St. Wilfred's C of E Secondary School retained its 11–18 status. Taken together with the now independent Queen Elizabeth's Grammar School and the independent Westholme Girls School, sixth form provision in the borough became fragmented. The existence of church and independent schools, with their own admissions policies, also resulted in the mainly Muslim ethnic minority children being unequally distributed amongst Blackburn's secondary schools.

At the Technical College the new Feilden Street building was completed in 1964, but further building was halted when the Harris College in Preston was chosen for Polytechnic status in preference to Blackburn. This was yet another sign of Blackburn's declining local importance. The next phase of building came in the 1980s when it became a tertiary college. A campus site was formed between Feilden Street, Nab Lane and Blakey Moor and a series of new buildings erected, including a new Art and Design School and a New Technology Centre. In addition the older buildings were refurbished. The institution was renamed, and Blackburn College came into existence. The plans for adult education in community centres on the new housing estates, however, never came to fruition.

One further change that Blackburn experienced in the post-war years was the influx of large scale immigration of families with Indian or Pakistani ethnic origins. The motives for this immigration are much the same as those which drove the Irish immigrants in the nineteenth century. They were attracted by the lure of a comparatively better life with better paid employment. At home in India and Pakistan, population increases that brought fragmentation of agricultural holdings, together with a tradition of migration, helped fuel the exodus. This did not totally apply to those Asians that came via Africa. They were expelled, particularly from Uganda, or faced political uncertainty.[22]

Immigrants came from three main areas: the Gujarat State in India, the Punjab Province in Pakistan, and from Uganda, Kenya, Malawi and Tanzania in East Africa. 89% were Muslim, 8% Hindu and 1% Sikh.[23] The majority came from India and from a rural background.

Blackburn experienced a large influx of Asian immigrants in the 1960s and 1970s. Like the Irish in the nineteenth century, these new immigrants found themselves in low paid employment and consequently settled in the older areas of the town where cheaper property was available to satisfy their desire to own their own home. One result for Blackburn has been the building of a number of mosques to add to the religious architecture of the town. This photograph also shows how the town centre is dominated by the graceless stump of the Town Hall Extension.

Photo by Ian Beesley

Table 4   Background of main Asian immigrant groups in Blackburn.[24]

Rural Indian Gujarati Muslims	29.7%
Rural Pakistani Punjabi Muslims	21.2%
Urban Indian Gujarati Muslims	8.7%
Rural East African Gujarati Muslims	8.2%
Urban East African Gujarati Muslims	5.6%
Urban Pakistani Punjabi Muslims	5.5%

As with the Irish in the nineteenth century, most immigrants found themselves in low paid employment and consequently settled in the older areas of Blackburn. In this case it was in order to purchase property cheaply rather than rent it. This certainly altered the proportion of owner occupied property in the town. In 1977 owner occupation in the borough totalled 64.6%, a figure greatly enhanced by the fact that within the ethnic minority population it was 93%.[25]

They also tended to form their own isolated communities. These were divided on first arrival along national and religious lines, but divisions have been partly perpetuated by the way each community helps relatives, friends and past neighbours to settle and set up house on arrival in this country or on marriage. Because of this, Gujarati Hindus tend to live in streets around Preston New Road as do the Punjabi Sikh families. Gujarati Sunni Muslims, the largest ethnic group, live in the Brookhouse area especially in the south-west corner. The Gujarati Surtis group tend to live in the Daisyfield and Audley Range area. Pakistani Sunni Muslims live in the streets of the north-east corner of the Brookhouse area and in the Audley Range, Queen's Park and Green Bank areas.[26]

The number of ethnic Asian immigrants, however, far outstrips those of the nineteenth-century Irish in Blackburn.

Table 5   Total Asian Ethnic Immigrants in Blackburn

1951	287
1961	652
1971	5,355
1981	15,237
1990	19,300

This meant that in 1990 those with an Asian heritage made up nearly 15% of the population of the new borough of Blackburn and Darwen. It is set to grow even higher still. Adult Asians only make up 9.8% of the population whilst schoolchildren from Asian backgrounds make up 27% of the school population. This is largely the consequence of the young age of the immigrants, like most immigrants historically, who began families soon after arrival. The figures are higher for the old borough of Blackburn where the majority of the immigrant communities live. In terms of being home to the largest Asian settlements in the United Kingdom, Blackburn was 15th in 1971 and 12th in 1981.[27]

Most immigrants were attracted to Blackburn's textile industry. In 1977, when only 10.3% of the town's workforce was employed in textiles, 54.1% of all immigrant adults were thus employed.[28] The industry's constant decline has brought employment problems to Blackburn's ethnic minority community. When unemployment was 6.5% in the town in 1977, it was 21% amongst the Asian population. The same pattern persists today. Whilst Blackburn's unemployment rate in April 1990 was just under 8%, the rate in Cathedral ward, which has a large ethnic minority community, was over 17%. It was also over 15% in the Brookhouse, Bank Top and Queen's Park wards which also contain a high proportion of the local ethnic minority population.[29]

The relatively low paid work many of the immigrant community are employed in, coupled with the disproportionate number of them who are unemployed, means that the areas in which they live are amongst some of the most deprived in Blackburn. In 1984 a survey by the General Practitioners' Committee identified the Brookhouse and Cathedral wards as the two most deprived out of 9,200 in England and Wales. This came on top of a Department of the Environment survey, based on 1981 census information, that indicated that the Borough of Blackburn was one of the ten most deprived local authority areas in England and Wales.[30] Blackburn is still suffering from her nineteenth-century housing legacy and the collapse of the cotton industry.

Politics is yet another area in which the past still exerts a pull on the present. Blackburn remained a two-member constituency in 1945, and in the Labour landslide of that year the borough returned two Labour MPs including Barbara Castle, a future cabinet minister. The constituency was then divided into Blackburn East and Blackburn West. In the 1950 election Barbara Castle was returned in Blackburn East with a majority of 4,818, but Blackburn West fell to the Conservatives. The position remained the same in 1951 except that Barbara Castle's majority was reduced to 2,632. Because of Blackburn's declining population it now reverted to being a single constituency though this time with only a single seat. Barbara Castle hung on to it in 1955 but only with the very small majority of 489. Since then it has remained a Labour seat, Barbara Castle being succeeded by Jack Straw in 1979. Considering that Blackburn is a manufacturing town with a large working-class base, that it has experienced a larger than average

A young Barbara Castle campaigning in the 1945 General Election. After winning her seat in the Labour landslide victory of that year, Barbara Castle retained it until her retirement from Westminster in 1979. Though Blackburn was an industrial town with more than its fair share of housing and unemployment problems, the Labour Party's hold on the seat was often tenuous, reflecting Blackburn's still strong working-class Conservative support. *Courtesy of Blackburn Library*

unemployment rate, and that it has had Labour candidates in the cabinet and shadow cabinet, it is surprising that the Labour Party has had such small majorities. In 1970 Barbara Castle only retained her seat with a majority of 2,736 whilst Jack Straw had one of only 3,055 in 1983. Admittedly this has strengthened to 6,027 in 1992 though much of this is probably due to a growing personal vote that may not help his successor. Without the large ethnic minority vote they may well have been defeated on such occasions. Blackburn still retains a large, traditional, working-class Conservative vote. The brief prominence of the National Front and the National Party in Blackburn during the 1970s is partly evidence of this, though their ultimate failure was probably a testimony to the town's traditional antipathy to political extremism.

The saga started in 1971 with the 'Battle of Azalea Road'. It was alleged that residents were angered by the possibility of one of their neighbours selling their property to an Asian family. Immediately the National Front sent an organiser from the Manchester area to Blackburn. A local branch of the National Front was formed, and it was claimed that 'the rapid development of the Blackburn branch is the greatest success story in the Lancashire area to date'.[31] For some years, however, the National Front remained just an undercurrent in local politics. It was when a local man, Kingsley-Read, became one of the national leaders of the Front and then, in a much publicised split, led the new breakaway National Party of Great Britain, that extreme right-wing politics took on a higher profile in Blackburn.[32] In the 1975 Council elections, Kingsley-Read won a seat in St. Thomas's ward and John Franklin, a fellow member of the National Party, won one of the seats in St. Jude's ward.

The following months saw the media descend on Blackburn and the town hosted a series of marches and counter-marches organised by the National Front, the National Party and Action Against Racism.[33] The largest took place in September 1976. Organised by Action Against Racism, 3,500 took to the streets. But it was claimed by the Provost of Blackburn, the Very Reverend Lawrence Jackson, that the bulk of the marchers were not Blackburn people but outsiders bussed in from all over Britain. 'Blackburn people,' he claimed, 'were conspicuous by their absence and I think this was Blackburn's own demonstration of how they want to be left to be allowed to get on peacefully.' The Mayor agreed with this opinion, but in true nineteenth-century entrepreneurial spirit he mainly bemoaned 'the effect on trade in the town' and claimed that many shoppers had gone to Accrington for the day.[34]

The marches and demonstrations continued, though they grew sparser both in their number and in the crowds that they attracted. By May 1978, despite wide publicity before the event, a National Front march and a counter-demonstration went off 'like a damp squib'. Both sides added together totalled less than 1,000, and only one demonstrator got excited enough to get arrested.[35] Kingsley-Read failed to be re-elected to a second term of office, and Franklin had resigned even before attending a single council meeting. Though party internecine strife helped, it was mainly public apathy that killed off political extremism in Blackburn, just as it had seen off the Communists as well as Oswald Mosley and his Blackshirts in the interwar years.

During the second half of the twentieth century Blackburn has done much to try to escape from the legacy of its past. Much of it, however, tenaciously remains and still colours many areas of life. A good deal has been done in the area of housing improvements, but because most of the old housing stock was around the same age and quality, part of it was deteriorating just as quickly as other parts were being replaced or improved. Much of the nineteenth-century town centre has been swept away entirely, yet the new structures are in danger of being dated before their time. New industry has been attracted to replace cotton in the town's economy, yet higher than average unemployment persists. Because of such factors, deprivation is still experienced in many areas of the town. The result is a population that continues to decline notwithstanding large scale immigration. Blackburn had come to prominence through cotton. Now that cotton has gone Blackburn is finding it difficult to find a new *raison d'être*. It is still looking.

REFERENCES

1. Chronology of Air Raids near Blackburn 1939–45 in Blackburn Library Local History Collection.
2. *Blackburn Times*, 31 May 1940 and 27 September 1940.
3. *Blackburn Times*, 12 July 1940 and 1 August 1952; *Lancashire Evening Telegraph*, 5 February 1979; Mullards' Jubilee Pamphlet 1920–1970.
4. *Lancashire Evening Telegraph*, 16 July 1974, 5 February 1979 and 21 August 1980.
5. Mullards' Profile Pamphlet (1970); Mullards' Jubilee Pamphlet 1920–1970.
6. *Blackburn Times*, 1 August 1952; *Lancashire Evening Telegraph*, 24 April 1953, 3 December 1958 and 20 February 1959.
7. *Scapa News*, 40th Anniversary Issue 1927–1967.
8. Collection of Advertising Literature in Blackburn Library Local History Collection.
9. Brian Conduit, *Blackburn 1934–1987: Historical Summary for City Status Bid* (in author's possession); census statistics; *The Changing face of Blackburn and Darwen*, 2nd Edition, Blackburn and Darwen Borough Council, 1990.
10. Blackburn Borough Planning Department, *Blackburn Statistics* 1983.
11. *Blackburn Statistics* and *City Status Bid*.
12. N. Andrews, 'Housing obsolescence: a case study of housing renewal in Blackburn', BA Dissertation, Liverpool Polytechnic, 1981, pp.34–37.
13. Andrews, 'Housing obsolescence', pp.34–37; W.D. Hamilton, 'Survey of Blackburn's housing and factors affecting improvements or clearance', unpublished BA Dissertation in Blackburn Library Local History Collection; Census statistics 1971.
14. Andrews, 'Housing obsolescence', pp.36–37.
15. Blackburn Housing Department, 'Housing strategy statement and housing investment programme submission, 1991–92'.
16. Figures from The Chartered Institute of Public Finance and Accountancy, 1982 quoted in Vaughan Robinson, *Transients, Settlers and Refugees: Asians in Britain*, Clarendon Press, Oxford, 1986, p.222.

17. W. D. Hamilton, 'Survey of Blackburn housing and factors affecting improvement or clearance', BA Social Science project for unknown H. E. Institution, 1971; *Blackburn Statistics*; 'Housing Strategy Statement', p.7.

18. Ronalyn Hargreaves, 'The Changing Population of Blackburn 1861–1971', unpublished dissertation 1974, p.21, in Blackburn Library Local History Collection, and *City Status Bid*, p.9.

19. *City Status Bid*, p.6; Mary Smallbone, 'Blackburn Centre Redevelopment – Phase 11 Completed' in *Environment North West*, 23, January 1972.

20. *City Status Bid*, pp. 2, 4 and 7.

21. For most of the following facts see *City Status Bid*, pp 3–9.

22. Asian Household Survey Team, *Asians in Blackburn: The Socio-Economic Conditions of Blackburn's largest Ethnic Minority Grouping*, p.11, Blackburn Library Local History Collection; Robinson, *Transients, Settlers and Refugees*, pp.116–121.

23. Survey Team, *Asians in Blackburn*, p.11; Asian Household Survey Team, *Some Basic Characteristics of Blackburn's Asian Population*, p.24, Blackburn Library Local History Collection.

24. Robinson, *Transients, Settlers and Refugees*, p.239.

25. Survey Team, *Basic Characteristics*, p.41.

26. Rolf Erikson, *Survey of Ethnic Groups in Districts with Large Ethnic Populations in the County of Lancashire*, L.C.C Social Services Department 1987, pp. 82–102.

27. *Changing Face*, Section 5; Hargreaves, 'Changing Population'; Robinson, *Transients, Settlers and Refugees*, pp. 116 & 222.

28. Survey Team, *Basic Characteristics*, p.28.

29. *Changing Face*, Section 11; Conduit, *Historical Summary*, p.5.

30. Housing Department, *Housing Strategy Statement* p.2.

31. *Britain First*, Issue No.11, 2–15 October 1971; *Spearhead*, December 1971.

32. *Lancashire Evening Telegraph*, 30 December 1975.

33. *Lancashire Evening Telegraph*, 24 May 1976, 10 June 1976 and 11 September 1976.

34. *Lancashire Evening Telegraph*, 13 September 1976.

35. *Lancashire Evening Telegraph*, 13 September 1976.

FURTHER READING

W. A. Abram, *A History of Blackburn Parish*, J. G. & J. Toulmin, Blackburn, 1877.

J. J. Bagley and A. S. Lewis, *Lancashire at War: Cavaliers and Roundheads 1642–1651*, Dalesman Books, 1977.

D. R. Beattie, 'The Origins, Implementation and Legacy of the Addison Housing Act 1919, with special reference to Lancashire', unpublished PhD, Lancaster University, 1986.

S. P. Bell, *Victorian Lancashire*, David and Charles, Newton Abbott, 1974.

B. J. Biggs, 'Education in Blackburn 1870–1914', unpublished MEd., University of Durham, 1961.

C. Birtwistle, 'A History of the Education of Children in the Blackburn Hundred to 1870', unpublished MA, London University, 1952.

Alan Booth, 'Reform, Repression and Revolution: Radicalism and Loyalism in the North West of England 1789–1803', Unpublished PhD, Lancaster University, 1979.

Duncan Bythell, *The Handloom Weavers*, Cambridge University Press, Cambridge, 1969.

John Clay, 'The Tramways of Blackburn 1851–1949', unpublished BA, Lancashire Polytechnic, 1984.

Brenda Crosby, 'The Lancashire Campaign of the British Union of Fascists 1934–1935', unpublished MA, Lancaster University, 1977.

J. C. Doherty, 'Short-Distance Migration in Mid-Victorian Lancashire: Blackburn and Bolton 1851–1871', unpublished PhD, Lancaster University, 1985.

W. Durham, *History of Blackburn A.D. 317–1868*, Blackburn, 1868, reprinted by T.H.C.L. Books, 1988.

Mary Ellison, *Support for Secession: Lancashire and the American Civil War*, University of Chicago Press, Chicago and London, 1972.

J. H. Fox, 'The Social Origins, Careers and Characteristics of Entrepreneurs in South Lancashire During the Nineteenth Century', unpublished MA, Lancaster University, 1970.

D. S. Gadian, 'A Comparative Study of Popular Movements in North West Industrial Towns 1830–1850', unpublished PhD, Lancaster University, 1976.

A. Granath, 'The Irish in Mid Nineteenth-Century Lancashire', unpublished MA, Lancaster University, 1975.

W. A. Hamilton, *Remembering My Good Friends*, London, 1944.

D. J. Hill, 'The Growth of Working-Class Sport in Lancashire', unpublished MA, Lancaster University, 1975.

A. Howe, *The Cotton Masters 1830–1860*, Clarendon Press, Oxford, 1984.

Felicity Hunt (ed), *Lessons For Life: The Schooling of Girls and Women 1850–1950*, Basil Blackwell, Oxford, 1987.

Michael Jones, 'Deference and the Blackburn Working Class: Operatives Struggles 1852–1878', unpublished MA, Warwick University, 1984.

Patrick Joyce, *Work, Society and Politics*, Harvester Press, London, 1980.

Brian Lewis, *Life in a Cotton Town: Blackburn 1818–1848*, Carnegie Press, Preston, 1985.

R. A. Light, 'The Lancashire Power-Loom Breaking Riots of 1826', unpublished MA, Lancaster University, 1982.

Norman Longmate, *The Hungry Mills*, Temple Smith, London, 1978.

J. C. Lowe, 'Parliamentary Elections in Blackburn and the Blackburn Hundred 1865–1880', unpublished MLitt., Lancaster University, 1970.

J. D. Marshall, *Lancashire*, David and Charles, Newton Abbott, 1974.

Denise Martin, 'Women Without Work: Textile Weavers in North east Lancashire 1919–1939', unpublished MA, Lancaster University, 1985.

G. C. Miller, *Blackburn: Evolution of a Cotton Town*, Blackburn Town Council, Blackburn, 1951.

W. E. Moss, *Life of Mrs. Lewis*, London, 1926.

Pilgrim Trust, *Men Without Work*, Cambridge, 1938.

R. J. Poole, 'Wakes, Holidays and Pleasure Fairs in the Lancashire Cotton Districts c.1790–1890', unpublished PhD, Lancaster University, 1985.

Rex Pope, 'The Unemployment Problem in North East Lancashire 1920–1938', unpublished MLitt., Lancaster University, 1974.

M. Rothwell, *Industrial Heritage: A Guide to the Industrial Archaeology of Blackburn Part 1 The Textile Industry*, Hyndburn Local History Society, 1985.

M. Rothwell, *Industrial Heritage: A Guide to the Industrial Archaeology of Blackburn Part 2 Other Industries*, Hyndburn Local History Society, 1986.

Morris B. Smith, 'The Growth and Development of Popular Entertainment and Pastimes in Lancashire', unpublished MLitt., Lancaster University, 1970.

J. G. Timmins, 'The Decline of the Handloom Weavers in Nineteenth-Century Lancashire', unpublished PhD, Lancaster University, 1990.

G. N. Trodd, 'The Local Elite of Blackburn and the Response of the Working Class to its Social Control', unpublished MA, Lancaster University, 1974.

G. N. Trodd, 'Political Change and the Working Class in Blackburn and Burnley 1880–1914', unpublished PhD, Lancaster University, 1978.

D. Walsh, 'Working-Class Development, Control and New Conservatism: Blackburn 1820–1850', unpublished MA, Salford University, 1986.

P. A. Whittle, *Blackburn As It Is*, privately published, Preston, 1852.

J. C. Wilsher, 'Popular Literary Culture in a Nineteenth-Century Cotton Town: A Social Study of the Blackburn Poets', unpublished MA, Lancaster University, 1970.

188

190

191